Seth details his proce
and transparent mann
but through the lens of the entire family dynamic. He describes
grief from an experiential perspective that includes the shock
and pain and also the reliance of God, family, and pure faith to
rise above such tremendous loss. Seth takes us on a journey of
devastation and loss but also how he fostered an understanding
and acceptance for him, his children, and his family. He has
done so masterfully in a way that gives us all hope and increases
our faith in the power of love and the Lord.

—Jacqueline F. Coulter
LCMFT, LMFT

Grief is different for everyone, yet everyone goes through many
of the same processes. Tyler is raw, vulnerable, and relatable
as he walks through facing the truths of this most difficult life
challenge.

—Cheryl Botkins
LPC, MSCC, NBCC

This intensely personal account of an unthinkable situation
reveals the hopeful blessing Seth discovered despite deep pain
and loss. Prepare to join him there.

—Dr. David Fincher
president of Central Christian College of the Bible

A JOURNEY THROUGH UNEXPECTED LOSS

ABOUT THIS GRIEF

A widower's perspective on learning to grieve, heal, and help while trying to find peace in the middle of the storm and its aftermath

SETH TYLER

BROOKSTONE
PUBLISHING GROUP
Birmingham, Alabama

About This Grief

Brookstone Publishing Group
An imprint of Iron Stream Media
100 Missionary Ridge
Birmingham, AL 35242
IronStreamMedia.com

Library of Congress Control Number: 2022921388

Cover design by Hannah Linder Designs

ISBN: 978-1-949856-92-7 (paperback)
ISBN: 978-1-949856-93-4 (ebook)

1 2 3 4 5—27 26 25 24 23

For my boys.
May you always remember
that you are strong, brave, and loved!

CONTENTS

ACKNOWLEDGMENTS

There are many, many people who assisted, aided, and contributed to this book. From walking alongside us through tragedy or walking step-by-step through the writing of this book—there is no way that I could list out each person that has impacted our lives and the creation of this book. That won't stop me from trying though!

First and foremost, I have to thank my parents. There is absolutely no foreseeable way that I would be where I am without my parents coming to my side in the late hours of a dreadful night and remaining there indefinitely always willing to help. They have sacrificed and rearranged their lives in order to help when they didn't have to. Thank you, Mom and Dad! I pray that my boys know the love in their lives from me that I do daily from you.

Thanks to those who were there for me from the beginning. Specifically, thank you Ray and Tommy. Ray, thank you for staying on the phone for the entirety of that dreadful car ride to the hospital. You were the first to know of my loss and the first to console this grieving husband. Tommy, thank you for guiding me through the funeral process and in those first few days as a widower.

Thanks to my village. They say raising kids takes a village. I have needed a village to walk alongside me through my grief, help with my boys, and for a plethora of other reasons. If you have been at my side at any point through the tragedy and after, you are my village. Thank you to Northside Christian Church, member churches of WCCSC, and my friends and family who have simply showed up for us.

Thanks to those who believed in the project and helped in some form: Kylee, Ray, Jessica, and Chris for reading a jumbled mess of a first draft and giving feedback; my small group, family, and friends who helped me choose a cover design (and viewing modifications repeatedly); Crystal and Carl for believing in me and investing in me.

Thanks to the team at Iron Stream Media for their work on this book: Suzanne, thank you for meeting with a stranger to talk about a project because of a social media inbox message you received; John, thank you for assisting with the direction of the book. To Susan and her team for all things editing; Michele and her team for all things publishing; Bethany for helping me arrange my thoughts and enhancing my voice and message throughout.

Thanks to the board at West Central Christian Service Camp that has allowed me to be flexible in all things camp and life. This project is a by-product of your commitment to be there in our time of need. Thank you for the support, prayer, and care that you have given us.

Thank you to my terrific boys: Blake, Rhett, and Hunter for giving grace and being patient as Daddy works and writes. Blake, thank you for your awesome contribution to this project!

INTRODUCTION
ABOUT THIS BOOK

I'll start out by saying that I'm not a mental health professional and do not pretend to be one. What follows in this project is based solely on my personal opinions and what I have experienced through the unexpected loss of my beautiful wife, Carol. My desire is that you would experience hope in the midst of your own grief journey as you read about mine.

If there was one person who would have appreciated this book, it probably would have been Carol. She was such a kind and loving person. She dealt with a lifetime of anxiety, and with that comes a grief of its own and a deep compassion for others who are struggling. I know that she would have hated seeing us go through the deep sorrow of losing her, but the beauty of life and death in Christ is that this world is temporary. I know that I will be reunited with my wife someday, and we will share eternity in the presence of our Father in heaven.

I sincerely hope that you are helped by what we have been through. I'm not sure if we ever have finality or complete closure in times of loss, but we can have peace and comfort. I pray that as you read our story, you are equipped and empowered to bring honor to your loved one's life.

This is not a guide to grieving. I wish I could provide a guide with ten steps to healing, but our unexpected journey through grief has not been smooth. I can't offer an easy way through grief. What I can offer is my vulnerability and struggles through the grief process. I hope that as you learn about how I have failed and succeeded through the different seasons of grief, it may offer insight to healthy grief and mourning. The depths of grief that you may experience will undoubtedly feel like a weight on your shoulders, but I pray that the weight may feel a little lighter by reading this book.

Remember that you are not alone while you grieve, and I pray blessings over each person who reads of our journey. May you experience hope and overwhelming peace in your time of unimaginable loss.

This is for my boys so they understand who their mother was, whom she served, and how they can make it through hard things in life. I pray that they can look back on this later and be reminded that they are the strongest when they are within the body of Christ.

I write this for them and in honor of their mommy and my Carol.

You will keep in perfect peace
    those whose minds are steadfast,
    because they trust in you.
Trust in the LORD forever,
    for the LORD, the LORD himself, is the Rock eternal.

—Isaiah 26:3–4

CHAPTER 1
ABOUT THAT DAY

"I want to see Jesus, but I'm not sure I'm ready to right now."

A couple of hours before my wife shared this thought with me, I was outside mowing. Carol and I managed a church camp, sitting on roughly fourteen acres, in the middle of Missouri. The summer of 2021 was our first active summer because the previous year camps were shut down due to Covid-19 lockdowns. It was a Thursday evening, June 17, 2021. The Friday before, we had a very severe storm blow through and tear the property up, so we were working diligently to get the camp prepared for the following week of summer camp.

I was on the mower headed to a small piece of ground that needed to be mowed when Carol, who had been cleaning one of the dormitories, called me on the phone and told me to come over to her fast. She was feeling light-headed, like she was going to pass out, and was having some pain in her chest. I figured that riding the mower to her was going to be faster than shutting it down and running there, so I put the pedal to the metal and drove over to her. I found her outside, leaning on the Kawasaki Mule that the camp owns.

I asked her if she needed to go to the hospital, and she, without hesitation, said yes. This is when I realized that it was not a panic attack or anxiety related. She was sure what she wanted, so we got on the UTV and raced up to our house. I walked her to the SUV and opened the passenger-side door. I told her to get into the vehicle so I could go inside to retrieve the car keys. She began to get into the vehicle, so I rushed inside as she got situated. As I hurried to get the keys, I informed our summer nanny, Elleanna, who was in the living room with the boys, that I was taking Carol to the hospital.

Little did I, Elleanna, or the boys know that when Carol left the house an hour before to go clean the dorms, it would be the last time that Elleanna and the boys would see her alive. I understand that that is a terrifying thought, but it has been a reality that has changed how I leave people, what I say when I leave, and the smile that I leave them with as I go.

I made it back to the Durango and found Carol lying on the ground next to the SUV looking at the trees and the sky. When I went into the house for the keys, Carol decided to lie down next to the vehicle instead of getting in because she was dizzy. I didn't know at that time that she was lying there pondering if this was when she was going to see Jesus.

I helped her into her seat, and we were off to the hospital. What typically takes twenty-five minutes driving the speed limit did not take that long that night. It felt like an eternity, but it was definitely not twenty-five minutes.

As we were on the road, I called both sets of our parents. I didn't know what to do besides take her to the hospital, and on the way there, Carol began shutting down to deal with the pain and the anxiety that came with such an event. Her head and chest hurt and she had some tingling in her body. It hurt to speak, she wanted to vomit, and her vision was not normal. I was sure that she was having a heart attack. She breathed through it all and tried focusing her mind. She was as strong as I had ever seen her. I wasn't sure if she was going to pass out or what was to come. I just knew that I had to get to that hospital quickly.

Although Carol's symptoms looked and felt very serious on the way to the hospital, I'm not exaggerating when I say, by the time we made it to the hospital, she was *perfectly normal.* She even contemplated not going in. She thought they'd just say that it was a panic attack. She wasn't wrong, to an extent.

We went into the emergency room and didn't have to wait very long. I was still filling out some paperwork when they took her back and began working with her. By the time they let me back there with her, they had already checked her vitals, drawn some blood, done an ultrasound, and run an EKG. All her vitals were normal; her blood pressure, EKG, heart rate, and ultrasound were all fine. Carol told me that a nurse told her with a smile, "If you were any healthier, then you'd be sick." I wasn't exactly sure what she meant, but it came across that Carol was in great shape.

It was there at the hospital when no nurse or doctor was in her room that she told me that first line that you read. She explained what was going through her mind a few hours earlier as she laid by our SUV before we headed to the hospital. She said, "I just wanted to lie down. As I was lying there, I thought to myself, 'I want to see Jesus, but I'm not sure I'm ready to right now.'" That is when I knew just how serious and real that moment had been for Carol.

The nurse and doctor came back and told us that two of the blood components that they tested came back slightly elevated. They said it could be due to anxiety from the situation, but they wanted to run an echocardiogram to rule out a pulmonary embolism. They wanted to check for clots in her lungs. We said, "Yeah, do it. Let's rule it all out." Every decision we made was for her overall health and at the advice of the doctors. The results from the echocardiogram came back clear.

The one thing that kept us there in the hospital was the doctors' concern about elevated troponin in her blood. It could be evidence of a heart attack. They wanted to transfer her to another hospital that had a cardiologist on staff at night and had access to the equipment that might be needed. We asked them to transfer her to the best hospital that they knew of out of the list that they provided. This was all new territory for us, so we trusted their decision.

Out of the few things that I look back on and wished we had made a different decision about, this is one that I would have changed. In hindsight, we would have transferred to a different hospital. I can't change it. I accept that. That's the way life is. You make decisions, and you move forward with the outcome of those decisions.

The hospital staff told me that they would not allow me to ride with her by ambulance to the new hospital. They said that I would have time to go home and get a bag of essentials for us as it would take time for the paperwork and the transfer service to be set up. I drove home, making great time again, got the essentials for us, kissed the boys while they slept in their beds, and told Elleanna what was going on with Carol.

I flew back to the hospital just in time to make it to her room to see that she had been strapped to the transfer bed and was being pushed out of her ER room. It was then that I was told that the new hospital does not allow visitors to stay overnight, not even spouses. I knew I wasn't going to be able to ride in the ambulance, but now I wasn't even allowed to go inside the new hospital until morning.

I'm glad that I was able to make it back in time while they transferred her as it was the second-to-last time that I would be able to kiss her, hold her hand for a moment, and take care of and provide for her—even if it was just a small go bag for the hospital.

I watched the ambulance take off and leave for the new hospital. Later, I found a picture on her phone that she took from the back of the ambulance as she was lying on the bed looking toward the back doors.

I made my way back home, took a shower, and laid down. I texted Carol at 1:30 a.m. Here's our conversation:

1:30 a.m.
Me:
Are you there yet?

Carol:
Not yet.

Me:
Call or text me anytime. My guess is that they'll get you set up for the night once you're there. Maybe they'll go ahead and run tests. Try to write things down. Different tests and such and why and what they are testing for. You're doing great! I love you!

1:56 a.m.
Carol:
I'm in my room now.

Me:
Good. Are they going to let you rest?

2:44 a.m.
Carol:
I'm sure they will. They are still just checking vitals and
asking questions. I just did that stupid Covid test. I hated it.

5:17 a.m.
Carol:
Don't forget the goats before you leave.

5:55 a.m.
Me:
OK. Get any sleep?

I left our house that next morning, Friday the 18th, and made
the one-and-a-half-hour trip to the new hospital. As I got to the
hospital, I was able to find a parking spot close to the doors, and
then I found my way to her room pretty easily. I really do wish
that I could have stayed with her that previous night. I know I
couldn't control that, but just that extra bit of time would have
been great. To have had that extra few hours to talk would mean
the world to me now.

I was able to spend about an hour with her or maybe a little
more on that Friday morning. Had I known that was the last
time that I would hold her hand, kiss her, hear her talk to the
boys, or hear her voice, I would've given 1,000 percent to that
one hour. Don't get me wrong—I was present and with her
the whole time; I just would have tried to remember every last
second of it had I known. Most times we don't get to know that
kind of thing, and that's OK.

In that hour together we talked to the doctor, called the boys,
and talked with each other. She was scared. Who wouldn't have
been in that situation? To be, by all accounts, a healthy individual
and then not know what was going on at all would be scary.

The doctor came in and informed us that they wanted to do a coronary angiogram, also known as a heart cath, to be sure that there were no blockages in her arteries. They also wanted to do another ultrasound to see if anything had changed since the one performed at the first hospital. If it was safe and going to rule out bad stuff, we were for it.

The ultrasound staff eventually came in to take Carol back. I told her, "Have fun. I love you. I'll see you later."

Those were the last words that I spoke to Carol while she was awake. She left that hospital room in no pain, with excellent vitals, and in good spirits.

While Carol was back with them doing the tests, several people came into the room where I was waiting. First, someone came in to take Carol back for the heart cath only to find that she was with the ultrasound team. Then, a hospitality lady came into the room to make sure things were good. Another woman came into the room to see if we were going to need financial assistance. It wasn't until after the financial assistance lady left that things got weird.

The strangest exchange I had with someone coming into the room once Carol had left for her tests was with a cleaning lady who came in and went into the bathroom and then appeared to be cleaning the room that I was sitting in—the same room where we had our stuff sprawled about.

The cleaning lady said, "Oh, are you in here? I thought they had you transferred to ICU."

"No," I said. "They just took my wife back for a couple of tests a little while ago."

The cleaning lady said nothing and left the room. *Well, that was strange*, I thought to myself.

Immediately after the cleaning lady left a nurse came into our room.

"There was a complication in the heart catheter procedure, and the doctor will be in soon to explain." That was all she said, and then she left the room.

Quietly panicking, I knew in that moment that I needed to prepare for something that wasn't going to be good news. I packed our stuff up quickly and awaited the doctor's explanation.

After about ten minutes, the doctor came into the room. I was sitting in the guest chair of the room nervously tapping my foot. Why I remember that, I don't know. He grabbed what I call the "doctor chair" and sat down. He explained that during the procedure there was a complication. The good news was that there were no blockages, but the bad news was something he called a "dissection" of an artery wall. He drew me a picture and explained that the dissection, or tear, tore backward and then into another artery. The tear caused another massive tear, and those tears tore backward, causing an artery or arteries to fold in on themselves and block flow. He told me that during the procedure Carol had cardiac arrest. It sounded crazy to me because she went into the procedure to check for blockages, and they found no blockages, but while she was on the table in their care, blockages formed due to tears and complications. It was a bit ironic.

During that cardiac arrest event, Carol's heart function had been as low as 5 to 10 percent. They told me that it was good that it had happened on the table and not later as they were able to address the tears and problems within minutes. During this time, some fluid got into Carol's lungs, and they needed to address that at the same time as the other complications. They also dealt with a bleeding issue as they had her on some medication that prevented her blood from clotting quickly.

They had to insert stents and balloons into arteries of her heart and an Impella heart pump into her thigh in addition to performing CPR to help her get through this cardiac event. Without going into too much more detail, they struggled to keep her alive at that point, and she was in critical condition.

They finally got me to the waiting room for the cath lab. I waited, and I waited, and then I waited some more. I got up and looked for a bathroom, and I eventually just started opening doors that didn't have a passcode on them to see if I could find one. I made some phone calls. I put out prayer requests for Carol. I did what I thought I could do to help, but that wasn't much.

Finally, I was able to go back and speak with the surgeon, the one who performed the heart cath, and he told me that Carol had spontaneous coronary artery dissection or SCAD. SCAD is essentially one or many small tears in the artery walls of the heart. Many women in their forties and fifties deal with it; medication and other things can help with it, and they live their lives. For a thirty-four-year-old woman to have the worst-case scenario is a rare thing. The surgeon told me that Carol had the worst-case scenario and was in critical condition but had a strong heart. I couldn't figure out how those two went hand in hand. He didn't tell me just how serious her condition was on that table. I found that out later.

I was not able to see her for quite a while as the doctors and nurses were continuing to work with her and prepare her for transfer to an ICU room. A nurse came to me while I was in the waiting room and informed me that they would allow me to see her for a brief moment in the hallway before they transferred her to the ICU. I got to see Carol in the hallway just outside of the room where she went into cardiac arrest. She was sedated and unresponsive. She went into that procedure alert and able but left it on a bed strapped down and hooked up to multiple machines fighting for her life. It was so hard to see her like that. Tears filled my eyes, and my throat closed up as I bent down to give her a kiss on her forehead. I told her that she was a fighter and that they were taking care of her. I told her to be strong, to fight, and I repeated that I loved her. I tried not to cry. I don't think that she could hear me. Then they wheeled her away to her ICU room. I had to wait even longer to go see her in her room. I made camp in a new waiting room outside the ICU and was joined by Carol's parents.

The hospital staff told us that it would take an hour or a little longer to have Carol situated in her new room. We filled the wait time with small talk. What else can you do in a time of shock and disbelief? I made it back to the ICU waiting room, and they came and let me know that we, Carol's mother and I, could go see Carol. She was still sedated. In fact, she was never off sedation again. Every now and then, she would move and make a sound as if she wanted all the tubes and IVs out, but I was told that she was not awake. I know the sedation was for her good, but maybe we would have been able to communicate with each other one last time had she not been sedated. That didn't happen. I held her hand. I talked to her. I talked to the nurses. They told me that she was doing well, that her vitals were getting better and looking good and that she simply needed rest. We filled out a contact form with my contact info, Carol's phone number (I had her phone with me), and both of Carol's parents' phone numbers. They put it with Carol's charts and files.

I left to let Carol's father come in to visit as they allowed only two visitors per patient. I went to the hospital cafeteria to try to eat a bite and see my family, who had come to the hospital. I tried to eat, but I hadn't cried yet, and all my body could do was cry at that point. So, I cried right there in the cafeteria with my family not knowing how to respond.

I made my way back to Carol's room and found that the nurses were encouraged by her vitals, and her oxygen level was good even though the amount given to her had been reduced. Her heart rate was a little elevated, but they thought that the breathing tube could be removed that same night or the next day. I was told that we could maybe even have Carol out of the ICU the following day. It was a long shot, but it was still encouraging to hear it was a possibility. I was then told that I could not stay overnight due to their policy.

Hearing that I couldn't stay overnight was difficult. I was torn between just getting a hotel nearby or going home for the night to see the boys. After the nurse said that it may serve the boys best to go home and see them and that Carol just needed rest, I compromised and elected to go home to see the boys for a few minutes, make sure my camp help had what they needed, and then come back and get a hotel room nearby. This decision was made only after I verified that they would contact me with any new information concerning Carol.

I left the hospital around 6:30 p.m. I got home around 7:50 p.m., saw the boys, spoke with my fill-in for work, and then sat down to have a conversation with my nine-year-old son about Mommy. It was during that conversation with my son that I received a call at 9:54 p.m. from the hospital that Carol was in cardiac arrest and that she had been intubated and they had been doing compressions for twenty minutes. I asked them to keep working on her, and the hospital assured me that they would.

I left my son without finishing our conversation, saying that I just needed to go see Mommy. At 10:10 p.m., the hospital called and said that they were taking Carol to the operating room for emergency open-heart surgery to try to help her. At 10:41 p.m., the doctor called and said that he had called it. He said that he would stay around and meet with me when I arrived. My heart shattered. I wasn't speeding anymore. I didn't want it to be true. It couldn't be true.

I was about fifteen to twenty minutes from getting to the hospital in time to see her while she was still alive.

At 11:05 p.m. I walked inside the hospital. There were a few people there in the lobby, and I wasn't getting anywhere with the receptionist. I told her my situation, and she called the ICU but got nothing in response. Someone nearby said something to me, and I thought it was a worker. I jumped on her a little saying, "My wife just died here, and I need to go see her." It wasn't an employee but someone else just trying to go in and see a loved one. She left the lobby and went outside upset. I feel bad about that. Someone else was going through something, and I made it worse. They didn't know my situation, and I made their situation worse. I regret that.

In times of shock, I believe we can lose ourselves a little. We don't want that to be the case, but in times of raw reaction that fight, flight, or freeze mode kicks in, and I wanted to fight. I wanted to fight to be by my wife's side as I felt that I was stripped of that by having to leave the hospital earlier that night due to the hospital's policy. I was wrong to lash out, and I wish that I could've been a better example of who I believe that I am, but that's not the way it unfolded. I've had to learn to give myself grace and understanding for that moment. It was not that woman's fault that my wife was no longer living. The hospital's policy was not her fault. It was not her fault that I lived that far away from the hospital. Sometimes, we don't know who to blame in our difficult times, so we lash out at anyone within striking distance, and my words hurt that woman. I pray that my actions going forward in times of struggle and hurt will be different and filled with grace and understanding of others' circumstances.

The receptionist still couldn't get the ICU nurses to answer the phone, so I called the doctor on his cell phone. He met me and took me back to the ICU. He let me know that when he left the hospital at 7:00 p.m. for the evening everything was good. He said at 8:00 p.m., the ICU nurses called him saying that they were trying to resuscitate Carol and that they had to do that at least two or three times. This was news to me as I didn't receive a call until two hours (9:54 p.m.) after they had resuscitated her at least a couple of times. I asked point-blank questions on why they hadn't called me until two hours had passed.

No one had answers for me at that time.

When I was able to talk to the nurse on duty, she said that she was not the one calling as she was helping with Carol. She pulled up the number that they did call, and it was one digit off from my cell phone number. They put the number in their computer wrong. They also had no answers as to why they didn't call the next three phone numbers on the contact info form.

I was able to spend some time in that room with Carol. It didn't feel as if she had died. It felt as if she were just sleeping. I wished it was just a bad joke, a way for them to get around the system to let me be there overnight, but it wasn't. To be extremely honest, that time with Carol is one of the memories that I think back on the most when I think of the entire event. I don't know if that is intentional. Maybe it's easier to remember her in that bed as just sleeping rather than the memories of her at the funeral. I held her hand. I kissed her head. The smell of her shampoo I remember still to this very moment. I just sat there holding her hand, not knowing what to do. How do you say goodbye to the love of your life? How do you go home knowing that your time on this earth now goes on without her? How do you tell your boys that their mommy is in heaven?

The one person whom I needed to make it through this event in my life was no longer living.

I'm trying not to cry in this coffee shop as I remember the events of the day that changed my life forever. I was so confused as to what had happened. The hospital said that they do more than nine hundred heart caths a year and that the chance of any complication was one in one thousand. Even at that, a complication does not equate to death. I was confused, angry, and worn down, not knowing how to respond.

I drove home with my father instead of my wife in the passenger seat in those early hours of the morning. I have video footage of me entering my home after we made it home from the hospital. I look dazed and confused. In a matter of just over twenty-four hours from when we went to the first hospital, I had become a widower, a single father of three with the weight of the world on my shoulders and no idea how to cope.

Reflection: God Met Me

The nightmare that I was experiencing had every piece in place to destroy me and send me into a tailspin of destruction. I'm so very thankful that people surrounded me in what was the darkest day and weeks of my life. Even though that day my world was completely shattered, and I felt like giving up, God met me in my time of despair. God is not far from you either. May you be surrounded with God's presence. May the light of His love and provision overwhelm you and keep you in times of darkness. May your eyes be open to His workings in your circumstances.

I remember my affliction and my wandering,
the bitterness and the gall.
I well remember them,
and my soul is downcast within me.
Yet this I call to mind
and therefore I have hope:

Because of the LORD's great love we are not consumed,
for his compassions never fail.
They are new every morning;
great is your faithfulness.
I say to myself, "The LORD is my portion;
therefore I will wait for him."

The LORD is good to those whose hope is in him,
to the one who seeks him;
it is good to wait quietly
for the salvation of the LORD.

—Lamentations 3:19–26

CHAPTER 2
ABOUT HER

Carol was a kind, honest, loving, courageous, and generous soul. As she got older, she began to realize her talents, her gifts, and the things that she was capable of doing.

We first met in the spring of 2007 at Central Christian College of the Bible in Missouri. She had just transferred to the college that semester. I had started back at the school for a second time in the fall semester of 2006 in pursuit of finishing my bachelor's degree.

Returning to this college in 2006 was probably one of the final pieces to ending the rough relationship that I was in before Carol's and my relationship. Looking back on it, that was hard to go through, but God found a way to make good out of it. Never have I been so blessed as I was by Carol coming into my life. We just hung out and got to know each other at first. By the fall semester of 2007, we were official. By the spring of 2008, I knew what I wanted. I wanted to marry her.

We spent most of our time together. I found, and this was obvious to anyone who had ever met her, that Carol was quiet, but, dang, was she kind. She had a soft voice, but over the years she found that voice, and it became stronger. Her heart was for people, and she would smile at everyone. Carol desperately wanted to serve people but struggled to find her way of doing so initially.

I found a social media post from when she was first learning how to crochet while I was at work. I had graduated with my bachelor of science in Christian education in 2008 and took a job teaching at a Christian academy that following fall. During the daytime while I was teaching, Carol began working on her craft of being extremely crafty. It was in those early years of marriage that Carol began to learn how to serve others through her own ministry of creating.

Carol was a baker, knitter, crocheter, painter, drawer, crafter, art journalist, and writer. She often downplayed her abilities in doing those things, but they brought such joy to so many around her.

Carol was a behind-the-scenes server of people, yet her love of Christ is now on display for all to see. My mission has been to have her legacy be as loud as possible. I feel that the best way to describe who Carol was is by sharing some stories about her.

The Interview

Carol dealt with anxiety her entire life. As I said earlier, her voice was soft, her manner was quiet, and she had a heart as big as the universe, but she didn't know how to express that completely because her anxiety was so strong. Panic attacks have a way of taking over, and the fear of having a panic attack may be just as crippling. Anxiety can be paralyzing and draining and can create a fear within that you believe you are not capable of doing the things that need to be done. I remember vividly the moment that I first saw Carol take an outward step in overcoming anxiety.

Carol did not like getting in front of people or being put on the spot. She didn't like to have to make those big decisions.

She wanted to be prepared for questions that might be asked of her. She studied the scripture before a Bible study so that she would know how to respond. She wrote things down so when she did have to answer, she'd have her cheat sheet. It's just how she worked.

I'll get back to the story. I was up for a position at a church and had done much of the hiring process. I still had an interview with some of the leaders, elders, and hiring committee members, and they asked Carol to be in there as well. She was not up for the position, and she was expecting to just be in attendance and not actively participating in the process.

A question was directed at me, and I answered it for them. I don't remember the specific question, but I do remember that after asking me, they directed the same question to Carol. The room was silent. Then, suddenly, I heard Carol speak from the heart. I remember being so proud of her in that moment for overcoming the anxiety of being put on the spot.

I knew at that moment that we were supposed to be at that church if that door was officially opened to us. I also knew that Carol's support of me was so strong that she would tackle her fear, panic, and anxiety to assist me. There were a few moments in ministry when I knew, very specifically, what the answer was or which direction we needed to go solely because of how Carol responded to something.

Although Carol might not have spoken much at Bible studies or in a group of people she didn't know, when she spoke, it was honest, kind, and what was needed.

The Birth of Blake
"I don't want to cuss!"

That is what Carol said to me as she was about to deliver our firstborn. There was a terrified look in her eyes, a fear of the unknown. I saw that look only four times in our entire time together—each time that she gave birth to one of our boys and then that Thursday night that I took her to the emergency room. It was a look like no other, a look that was part pleading for help and part terror mixed in with an "I don't want to do this." But she did do it.

I'll back up and give the whole story.

On Christmas Eve of 2008, just a few short months after we were married, we decided to start trying for a baby. It was then that we said that we were ready, but I'm not so sure that we knew what that meant. We tried for three years to get pregnant, and something just wasn't working. Believe me, it wasn't for a lack of effort! Those three long years felt like forever. We didn't even have those times where we thought she might be pregnant. It just wasn't happening. I do believe God was setting us up for the right place and time to have a child. During those three years, I was teaching at a small Christian school, and we were not making very much financially. I loved teaching at that school, and we didn't care that we didn't have much. We had each other, and that was all that we needed to get by. It helped that I was also working at a church each weekend, which gave us another part-time wage.

While teaching at the academy, the call to full-time church ministry had been growing within. After a couple of years, we transitioned to a midsize church in southern Missouri; it was in the middle of the country and drew people from thirty minutes away in every direction. I loved the people at that church, some of whom came to Carol's funeral even after all those years. I cried when I saw them. One evening at a church leadership meeting I told the leaders that we were trying to get pregnant and that we had been struggling with it for years. That night, those leaders prayed over our situation. One month later, we found out that Carol was pregnant. The power of prayer is something that can overwhelm any situation and bring forth the power of God.

Almost eight months later, we were sleeping in on a lazy day.

Carol said, "Seth, get up. My water just broke."

"No way," I said. "You probably just peed."

"Seth, we gotta go. Get up."

We didn't have any "baby go bags" ready. (Although we did have "tornado go bags" ready. We lived near Joplin, Missouri, at the time and had witnessed firsthand the destruction a tornado can bring.)

Let's get back to the birth story. We still had a couple of weeks to plan for our child to be born . . . or so we thought. Nonetheless, we were really excited, and as we got up, we remembered that just a couple of days earlier I had sprained my ankle very badly. Now, I had some good pain medicine, but the rush of her water breaking made me forget about my sprained ankle, and I shot up out of bed recklessly. When I went to put my legs to the side of the bed quickly, I bumped my leg, and I remembered rather painfully that I was injured. We grabbed my crutches and a couple of other things and made our way to the hospital just a few blocks away. Somehow, we ended up with a bag full of ketchup bottles that was still in our trunk from an event that we had just had at church. We were a mess.

I think Carol was taking care of me during this process. We got to the hospital and were set up in a massive room.

As the doctors and nurses all began to do their thing, Carol started to fret and get nervous. It was happening. We were about to no longer be just Seth and Carol; we were about to be Seth and Carol and baby. We were going to be responsible for another human, which is pretty crazy! You should have seen us in that hospital. I'm not sure what others thought of us, but we had to look kind of pitiful. Carol was lying in the bed in her hospital gown with doctors and nurses poking around, and then there I was, sitting in the recliner with my very sprained and very swollen ankle propped up and being iced often. I even asked her doctor once she was done helping Carol if she'd also take a look at my ankle. I laugh at the images in my head of how pathetic we must have looked.

At one point they wanted her to walk the halls to speed up the labor process. She obviously didn't want to do that alone, and her parents hadn't gotten there yet as they lived out of state. So, we asked if I could use one of the hospital's wheelchairs. There we were, making our way down the hospital hallways with her one hand on an IV tree as she worked that penguin wobble while I slowly rolled beside her in my hospital wheelchair with my leg propped up. I wasn't much help to her except for maybe a laugh or two.

The time finally came for her to start pushing. It was then that she looked at me with that look of terror and said, "I don't want to cuss." I couldn't keep from smiling. That was Carol. She wanted to do good by others, by the God she served, and by the standards that she kept for herself. She didn't want to cuss even when anyone in that position, any doctor, nurse, mother, father, minister, rabbi, or maybe even the pope would be like, "Nah, it's cool."

I miss that level of standard that she had for herself. When she was convicted of something, she tried to better herself no matter what it was. I learned from that just as much as she bettered herself by it.

Our room was situated near the waiting room, and we soon found out that the waiting room could hear quite a bit of what was going on in the labor and delivery room. The labor process started out quite normally. A couple of nurses, the doctor, her mother, and I were in the room. All of a sudden, though, another nurse would come in when the yelling got louder. When I say that she was yelling, it was YELLING! The waiting room could hear all of it. This was not the Carol you normally heard; she was such a quiet person. After one extra nurse came in, another person curiously followed. She wasn't a nurse but a hospitality worker. Then two more nurses came into the room. I remember trying to do my best for Carol by talking to her and just being there for her while trying to watch it all happen. I looked at her eyes, and she looked at me and then at all the people in the room staring at her with her legs up, fully exposed. She glanced back at me, and without saying a word, it was like we had a private conversation where we asked each other, "What is going on?!"

This event, the birth of Blake, was her most vulnerable moment up to that point in her life, and people were walking in like they had bought tickets at the theater and were ready for the show to start. The yelling and pushing continued, and more people probably crowded in for the show, and then it happened. The popcorn had been popped, the seats were filled up, and we were no longer watching previews. Our baby, Blake, entered the world and changed our lives forever. I never saw anything so terrifying, so gross, so amazing, and so wonderful all at the same time as when my child was born. I could have done without a lot of the birth parts, but sometimes going through the hard parts makes us appreciate the blessings the most. I will say that what we spouses see during the birth process never leaves the collection of images that take root in our internal photo gallery, but I wouldn't change that either.

Carol's strength and physical capacity to withstand delivery multiple times is beyond any strength that I could ever muster. Her mental fortitude to do what was necessary, even in the times that she didn't want to, was so strong. In that moment I saw the strength and power that she possessed that I had never seen before in those three years. I believe that is when she started to realize that she could do hard things.

And for those wondering, she didn't cuss.

Art Journaling

Carol was an excellent fiber artist. She could do anything fiber related with the best of them. She also taught herself many years ago how to do it all. I think she took one intro to crochet class and then taught herself everything else from knitting (her favorite) to fiber dying, cleaning, carding, spinning, and whatever other parts of the process there are that I can't remember. When news spread of Carol's passing, many people told me that they went right to the gift that she had given them or something that they had purchased from her. She put so much love and care into her craft and was so good at it.

I still have one of the very first things that Carol made—a little stuffed panda. It looks a little wonky and like a newbie made it, but she was so proud of it. She made it for a live benefit auction that the school that I taught at put on each year. When we were at the auction, no one was bidding on it, which I think was discouraging for her. We were newly married; she was staying at home at the time and just trying to figure out her talents, marriage, and all the things that come with being in a new place. She found something that she loved doing, and then she saw her creation sitting there not being cherished by a kid as she hoped it would. No grandparent even went over and put a bid on it.

Eventually, one person did put a bid on it. It wasn't me. It was my mom.

Even though my mom tried to keep it a secret, Carol knew. My mom will probably still deny it to this day, and if it truly wasn't my mother, then this worked out even better. It sold that night for the one bid that was written next to it.

Sometime later we visited a favorite local thrift store, and as we were going through the shelves, guess what Carol found! She found that wonky little panda, and she bought it. It could have been a thousand dollars, and she would have gone out and signed for a loan to buy it. That panda now sits on a shelf in our boys' room.

Carol came a long way from that beginner level and kept trying new things and found that new talents began to emerge. One time, Carol was asked to lead an art journaling class at a camp. She was so nervous, but man, did she do a great job with it!

Carol was an introvert; getting in front of people and speaking, teaching, or leading was daunting for her. She once told me that she had to give a presentation in school about something of her choosing. She had hamsters at home and decided she would give a presentation about hamsters. She worked hard on that presentation, but as it came to be her time in class to give her oral presentation, she forgot everything. Once she got up there in front of everyone, she panicked. She showed a picture or two, mumbled a couple of sentences and then showed them a live hamster. She said the teacher felt so bad for her that she gave Carol a passing grade.

I'm sure it goes without saying that when Carol was approached about leading this art journaling class at camp, she was petrified. The memory of that hamster presentation filled her mind. To my excitement, however, she said that she wanted to do it. She wanted the class to be excellent, so she planned and planned. She came up with an example of what the students could do and searched for Bible verse after Bible verse to use for the students. She wanted to feel comfortable up there, so she memorized every bit of what she wanted to explain to them and how to guide them in doing it.

The time came for the class to start, and I was her helper. She was so nervous but did such an awesome job. Carol had the students pick from a couple of Bible verses that she had written out and then asked them to meditate on these verses and what the verses led them to think about artistically. If a verse talked about God's power, then maybe they thought of thunder and lightning and could paint that. If a verse talked about God's creation, then maybe it had them thinking about mountains or a sunset in the horizon and they could paint that. And then, while painting, drawing, or sketching, they memorized and meditated on their verses. Carol memorized a lot of scripture this same way.

I think Carol had always thought that she couldn't bring the gospel to strangers or lead anyone to a deeper relationship with God without having a one-on-one relationship with them first because she was an introvert. However, she found that through her talents as an artist, knitter, crocheter, yarn dyer and spinner, art journalist, scripture journalist, mother, wife, and friend, she could have an impact on those around her. Even in death, she still has an impact on others, and I believe people will, for years and years, think about her and her impact on them as a friend and how she challenged them to grow deeper in their faith.

Carol's Obituary

I also believe Carol's obituary gave a beautiful example of who she was.

Carol Anne Tyler was born on September 30, 1986, in Memphis, Tennessee to Kevin and Wanda Crowe. The family moved to Missouri in 1990. Carol graduated from Bowling Green High School in 2005.

She met the love of her life, Seth, at Central Christian College of the Bible in 2007. They were married the next year on August 9 and had three boys together: Blake Daniel, Rhett James, and Hunter Warren. Carol was a stay-at-home mother, loving the time she was able to devote to her boys and her husband. They ministered in several churches in Missouri and Illinois until they found their dream job, becoming the camp managers of West Central Christian Service Camp in 2020.

Carol was very artistic and used her creative skills in her devotions with the Lord and in decorating their home and life. She especially enjoyed crafting, knitting, crocheting, painting and drawing. She shared her talents with others in different settings and taught on occasion. Carol loved living in the country and took great pleasure in watching sunflowers bloom. She was a faithful follower of Christ and trusted Him with her life unconditionally.

Carol passed away unexpectedly at the age of 34 on Friday, June 18, 2021.

Carol married into a large family that loved her and accepted her as well, considering her their own daughter and sister. In addition to the family that she was born into and the one she married into, Carol was loved by many friends who thought of her as family. Her encouraging words and caring spirit endeared her to many who will miss her greatly on earth."[1]

Reflection: A Legacy Left

It's important to me to highlight Carol's legacy, but I realize she is not the first to leave a legacy of love and kindness. She's not the first to show generosity, courage, and gentleness to others. She is not the first to leave a legacy worth writing about either. What about your loved one? What did they leave behind that you could hold on to and bring forth to others? How did they impact those around you, and how will you take their legacy and honor it in your own life?

It's comforting to look back on the time that I was able to spend with Carol and to write about her life. It brings hope. Reflecting on someone else's life allows us to put our own lives into perspective. What kind of legacy will we be leaving when our time on earth is done? I pray that my impact will be as Carol's was. I pray that my legacy will lead others to the glory of God as well.

My hope for you is that you will take some time to reflect on the life of your loved one. Write out their legacy. Find those stories that you've held on to and write them out. As you do, don't forget to have tissues by your side as it will be emotional. Don't be afraid of this time of reflection.

God is our refuge and strength,
    an ever-present help in trouble.
Therefore we will not fear, though the earth give way
    and the mountains fall into the heart of the sea,
though its waters roar and foam
    and the mountains quake with their surging.

—Psalm 46:1–3

CHAPTER 3
ABOUT THE KIDS

How do you tell a nine-year-old boy that his mom is not coming home? I know how I did, but I don't know the best way. There probably was a better way, but I couldn't think of any. Obviously, I had to tell him, but I didn't tell him immediately that next morning; I couldn't.

Blake had eaten breakfast already, and I had just woken up from the little sleep that I had gotten that night after getting home from the hospital in the early morning hours. First, I told our summer nanny and her friend, who had come down for the weekend, what had happened. I then went upstairs and asked Blake to take a walk with me. He said, "OK." He had no idea what I was about to tell him. He had no idea that I was about to crush him with the news he was about to hear. He had no idea that his naivete when it came to inner pain and hurt would be no more. Blake was going to have to learn life lessons that no young child should have to—how to deal with the death of a family member. The thought of his mother dying never once was expressed when she went to the hospital.

We walked a little bit on our way to the playground on the camp property. I hadn't said much yet. He knew nothing except that his mommy was at the hospital because her heart was sick.

That's what I had told him up to that point. We got to the playground area, and I sat with him on a bench inside the playground. I knew that I had to tell him. I knew inside that the news needed to come from me and not someone else.

"Blakey," I said, "I want to talk to you about Mommy."

"How is she doing? I know her heart has sickness."

"Yeah, you're right. Buddy, I don't know how to talk about any of this. Blakey, Mommy's heart was really sick, and she's now in heaven with Jesus."

"What?"

"Mommy is in heaven with Jesus."

"She died?!" He yelled loud enough to be heard across the camp property. Those two words still echo in my heart.

"I'm so sorry, buddy," I said. "I'm so sorry."

I remember his cries. I've never heard cries like that; they had such deep pain and sadness in them. I didn't know what to do, so we walked.

How I grieve is so different from how Blake grieves. How he grieves is so different from how the little ones grieve. While he grieves now, they will grieve later. I remember when my grandmother passed away. I was just a kid and not much older than Blake was when Carol passed. I remember not being able to withhold my crying at her funeral. I hear stories of my grandmother now from my father, and they bring her into a different light. It's almost as if I have a new memory of her. Death was such a hard thing to process as a child. Processing how someone can go from being with you to them being gone forever is difficult. I also remember when my oldest sister died in 2006. I struggled with her death. It weighed on me as a young adult and college student. She was diagnosed with a sickness, and the next month we were burying her. I don't have "new" memories of her, but I do now wish we had been able to make more memories. I mention these other women in my life because of the differences in how I dealt with each of their deaths due to my age and to show that we are affected differently by each death and event in our lives. It's not that you deal with tragedy better as you get older, but an understanding of life and death may allow us to process grief a little bit more easily.

It's very important that I show the boys that it is OK to deal with the loss of their mother. My desire is for them to do so in a healthy manner, and I believe that as they grow up, they will go through stages of grief. However, we are not waiting for the future to help them start processing their loss; we are working through the grief in the here and now. It poses the question: How have I helped my kids with their grieving process in the past, and how am I helping them now?

How I Handle the Grieving Process with My Kids

We talk. Carol, or Mommy, comes up often in our family conversations. With the little ones, it is mostly, "Mommy is in heaven with Jesus." They don't have the mental capacity to understand that Mommy is gone from this earth forever, but they do know that she is gone for now. That's OK. We still talk.

We ask questions. I ask the boys questions like these:

- What is your favorite memory of Mommy?
- What was the one thing that you always loved doing with Mommy?

- What was the funniest thing Mommy did?
- Do you remember when Mommy . . . ?
- How did Mommy make you feel when . . . ?

I try to keep the questions open-ended. Some of them are closed, but those responses lead to open-ended questions, such as "What was that like?" or "What about that did you like?" I want to keep the memory of Mommy alive even though she is not with us physically. Asking the boys questions is just half of it. The other half is that they feel comfortable asking me questions as well. I'll admit, I have yet to give every detail of their mother's death, but when they ask how she died, I give them an answer that I think they are capable of understanding. I have found it easiest to be honest with them. When they ask why she died, I answer that I don't know. I follow my answer with telling them that their mommy loved them very much, and I talk about how we have memories of Carol. I want them to be reminded that she loved them and of the time that they did get to spend with her.

We look at pictures. We look at pictures on the walls, on social media, from boxes of pictures. We point out and name each person in the picture ("Who is that? You're right. That's Mommy!"). We talk about what's taking place in the picture. Who is there? Why are we all there? Was that a fun experience? We look good, don't we? I also let them have pictures. I can always print more.

We do things that we did before she passed. We go to the same places to eat. We visit the same places that we've been before. We go and hang out with our friends. It isn't that we go do these same things to forget her, but we go and do these things because we have to be in action. We remember those special times and talk about them, but we also are making new memories.

Her family is still involved. Carol's side of the family is still our family. I can see how for some it would be easy to no longer see that side of the family simply for the case of awkwardness. However, the kids need that side of their family just as they need my side of the family. They get to see parts of Carol and parts of what made Carol, Carol. And her side of the family gets to see Carol in our boys.

I don't know what other people do in this situation, but I have made it very clear to each side of the family, my side and Carol's side, that the boys need to be a part of both sides and that doesn't stop because Carol isn't around.

Blake journals. Blake has a couple of different journals. He loves to draw, so one of his journals is specifically for drawing. The other is for when he reads his Bible. I give him freedom to do those things as he chooses.

He didn't journal right away. One night I heard some crying coming from his room. Now, we all have had our moments, but Blake has been so strong through this whole journey. He knows that he can cry at any point, ask questions, and come to me at any time. I think he's still learning how to grieve as well. I heard the crying while I was putting the two little ones down in their own beds. I walked into Blake's room, and he was weeping for his mother. It wasn't a cry because he scraped a knee or fell off his bike; it was an overwhelming sob from deep within crying out for his mother to hug him one last time. It was a cry from his heart needing his mother to come and comfort him. I know God took notice as one of His precious creations was in such sadness and despair.

Tears came down my own face as I was trying to be strong for him. I listened to him for quite some time as he cried out, wanting his mother. I held him. I put my hand on his back and answered questions as honestly and appropriately as I could to a ten-year-old child. He doesn't have to have every detail right now. He will in time, but in moments of such pain and anguish, too many details seem to make things murky and boil up already raw emotions.

That night, I simply mentioned to Blake that he should write about what he was feeling. It reminded me of a time that I told Carol the same thing.

When Carol and I were first married, we lived in a seven-hundred-square-foot apartment. It literally had a bedroom, an open kitchen/dining room/living room area, and an unusually large bathroom for that size apartment. We were in bed one night, and she began to have a panic attack. I was already asleep, and she woke me up from my sleep to tell me that she was nervous and was having a panic attack. I never fully woke up, but she said that I responded. (I'm sure there's a time that you can relate to that.) I responded with, "I think you should go write about it." She said it was just what she needed, and she did just that. Her journaling didn't really take shape or form that night, but she started to find ways to deal with her anxiety, panic attacks, and overwhelming emotions in those times. I'm so thankful that she did begin journaling as I can hear her thoughts, prayers, and voice through her Scripture journals and prayers still to this day.

Blake has taken that idea and run with it as well. I mentioned to him and only three other people at that time that I was working on a project and writing about my journey through this grief and asked him if he wanted to join in on the project. As long as he kept the project a secret, I was all for him being included in it. Why keep it a secret? Well, I wasn't sure at that time what I wanted to do with the project once completed. I didn't know if I was just writing this project out as part of my journey through grief and if I'd want to just have it for myself when it was done. I didn't want the added pressure of people asking about it, hence the secret. But I did definitely want Blake to be a part of it. You'll read his contribution to the book later in this chapter.

We find joy. It's hard for a ten-year-old to understand joy in the midst of trial. Let's be honest, it's hard for a thirty-eight-year-old to understand joy in the midst of trial. Losing Carol has been an absolute nightmare, yet we have found joy throughout our experience. Blake understands that more and more. It can be difficult to understand what Christians mean when we say that there is joy to be found in the middle of a trial. For some, I think it is just something that they say. For others, I honestly believe that they've been on their own grief journey, and they have found the times when joy has presented itself against all odds. It's like that plant that seems to find enough soil in the middle of a concrete sidewalk. There are still things to be joyful about even with the darkest clouds.

I was looking through pictures for much of the week after Carol died. Her parents also provided me with some pictures for the slideshow and to put on display alongside some of her art journaling projects on a table in the lobby. One picture in particular brought me joy. We always said that the boys look most like me and got their facial characteristics from me. That was, until I saw this picture. Now, our middle child had long, curly hair at the time. I looked at this picture of Carol as a child about the same age, and instantly I saw our middle child, Rhett. I couldn't unsee it. I see it more and more each and every day. It brought me joy. I smiled. I showed everyone around me Carol's picture compared to Rhett's picture. Even in my darkest week, I found that flower growing in the concrete world.

As the boys get older, I'm sure that I will continue to find more of Carol shining through them, and I hope that I do! We will continue to find joy on this journey of life as God leads us.

We cry. Not only is it OK for them to cry—it's OK for them to see me cry. I was never a crier, but now I find that I get choked up at a dumb, animated movie. I always thought it was weird seeing emotion from my parents when I was young. I've seen my dad cry a few times but usually only at funerals. I do remember seeing him cry in the hospital when I first broke down. Crying at a movie isn't something that I've seen him do. My mother, on the other hand, gets swept up in TV shows and movies. As kids, my brother and I would always point it out to her if we saw her showing emotion when watching TV. I'm not sure why we did it, but now that I find myself tearing up at an emotional part of a movie, I understand it a little more. Putting ourselves in the character's position is normal, but when our own loss is projected onto that character's circumstances, we feel the emotion on a different level. I decided early on not to hide my pain and tears after Carol passed. I want the boys to know, simply by seeing me being OK with it, that it is OK for them to show their emotions. The boys seeing me show emotion will open the door for them to feel comfortable emoting as well whenever they find themselves needing to do so. Having a healthy outlet for releasing emotion and inner turmoil is essential to healing.

We accept the fact that we all grieve differently. I envision that I will keep the same processes as we go forward. From personal experience, I know for myself that grieving takes many different forms. I do believe that it will be much different for the two little boys than it will be for both me and Blake. They were so young that they might have different feelings toward the whole thing.

When it comes time for them to grieve the loss of not having a mother during their formative years, their feelings might present as anger, rejection, and/or sadness. As they grow older and realize that Mommy is not coming home, they might bring up questions as to why they don't have a mommy and why Mommy isn't here. They might ask questions about why God took their mommy. They might be mad at Carol. They might get nervous and ask if God is going to take their daddy or even themselves as well.

We embrace our faith. I don't have the answers, and I never will. I know that the little boys' grieving is still to come, and I believe that how I handle my grieving and the process now can alleviate some of the weight that they'll feel later. Part of writing out our story is so that they can see later, when they are older, that Daddy still believes God has a purpose and that God still reigns. I deeply desire for them to know who Christ was to their mommy and who Christ is to me.

Knowing Christ brings peace and comfort.

May 18, 2021
Eleven months

It has been eleven months without Carol. We are quickly approaching the one-year anniversary of her death, and it feels like I can remember every detail as if it were yesterday.

This may be a strange thing to say, but it's weird not sharing a bed after so many years of doing so. It felt so empty at first. It still does . . . until the boys climb onto the bed in the middle of the night.

Last night was one of those nights. I was lying there thinking about how the next day was going to be eleven months since her death and was sad thinking about it. I heard one of the boys start to stir in the other room, and I quickly turned my light out so that they would think I was asleep and maybe would go back to sleep in their own bed. That didn't happen. Hunter got up and came into my room and climbed right onto my bed and snuggled right up close to me. I used to fight them coming into my room and climbing into bed, but I gave in, and my sleep has been so much better by not losing valuable sleep time trying to get them back in their bed and the battle that it is.

I started thinking as I laid there about why they come into the bed and concluded that they just want to be close to Daddy. They snuggle up because it's safe, comforting, and warm.

My mind went back to thinking about today and the eleven-month journey so far. That bed still feels unfamiliar being so empty and cold. You'd think that I would now use all of the bed at night, but I still sleep on "my side" where my wife's "side" of the bed remains empty.

While I was in my own thoughts, a little hand snuck into mine and just squeezed my hand, holding it tight. He didn't let go for some time until he was fully back to sleep.

I know what it's like losing a wife but not a mother. I can't imagine what it is like to lose your mommy at such a young age, even though he may not actually know it, but to know that for those few minutes I was able to make my youngest feel safe, warm, and comforted—it filled my heart.

I will never be able to provide the motherly care and love to him that he needs, but for last night and many nights now, I am glad for him and his brothers to warm that side of the bed to help them feel safe and comforted.

Our journey continues, and while we have sad moments and times when we need to feel safe and comforted, God finds a way to remind us to sneak our hand into His so we can hold on tight.

This next month will move fast, and I am unsure what that one-year anniversary will be like, but I know that the hands that made this world will gladly hold mine."[2]

ABOUT MOM
Written by Blake

Lord my God, I called to you for help,
 and you healed me.

—Psalm 30:2

Every now and then it just hits me very hard. Not long ago, it hit me so hard that she was gone that I cried for about forty minutes or so. That night, my dad (aka Seth) asked me if I wanted to go see my mom (aka Carol) at the gravesite after school the next day, and it made me feel good that he cares for me.

I was searching my Bible for comforting verses, and this is what I found:

"Have I not commanded you? Be strong and courageous. Do not be afraid; do not be discouraged, for the Lord your God will be with you wherever you go" (Joshua 1:9).

I also like Psalm 46:1–7. That one is too long to write, but while you are in Psalms, go to Psalm 56:3–4. It says,

When I am afraid, I put my trust in you.
 In God, whose word I praise—
in God I trust and am not afraid.

If you are worried because your person is very sick, read 1 Peter 5:7. It says, "Cast all your anxiety on him because he cares for you."

Maybe your person died, and you feel sad or alone. I've felt both of those things and at the same time. Remember, I am just a kid who is ten years old, and I lost my mom at a younger age than most people. I think about Psalm 34:18: "The Lord is close to the brokenhearted and saves those who are crushed in spirit."

I wanted to share some of the stuff that helps me feel comforted. Sometimes I listen to my mom's favorite band. I made them one of my favorite bands too. Also, I bring a stuffed animal with me when I stay the night somewhere else and even just around the house. His name is Sleepy. I have had him since I was two or three years old.

I miss a lot about my mom. I miss coloring with mom, and it was so much fun decorating Christmas cookies with her. Dad and I have a favorite saying that is like an inside joke with Mom. It was something she said on Christmas when she got some hair bands as a present. She said, "Oh yay, I needed these," but she said it in like a sarcastic voice even though she didn't mean to say it that way. We all laughed a lot about that. We still laugh about that.

Some of my favorite memories of my mom are when we hung out together. I liked drawing with her. I liked doing story time at night when I was young. I also liked when she read to me for homeschool, and I liked homeschooling with her. I liked when she was able to play too. We also made cookies a lot. It was fun!

When my mommy died, it was very hard. The night before she died, I thought, *She isn't going to die.* The next morning, my dad and I went to the playground, and he told me the bad, bad, bad, bad news that my mom died. My only mom died. That will probably be the saddest day of my childhood. Like I said in the beginning, sometimes it hits me, and I just cry hard. Toward the start of the school year, it hit really often, but now it doesn't hit as often. Just as I am writing this, a song came on the radio that made me emotional. Sometimes the lyrics to songs get to me and make me emotional, and I just sit and cry.

One more scripture that I like is John 14:18: "I will not leave you as orphans; I will come to you." I like that because Jesus tells His followers that He will always be there for them, and that is comforting to me.

Reflection: The Everlasting Father

My heart still aches for my boys, who have to grow up without their mother. I don't believe that there will be a day that I don't wish that they had her in their lives. What I do know is that they have a Father who will never leave them. I'm not talking about myself. There will be a day that I will no longer be around. Even when I am gone, they will still have a Father who deeply cares and yearns for them to be near to Him.

I can't think of a truer pursuit in my life than to lead my sons to the Father in heaven. I pray the same for you, to know Abba—God as Father. May the Father in heaven make Himself known to you in all seasons of your life. May you be overwhelmed by His presence. May His love overflow from you to your loved ones. May the Father's peace bring stillness and rest in your soul. I hope that as you walk through this journey that you do so hand in hand with the Father.

The Lord will fight for you; you need only to be still.

—Exodus 14:14

CHAPTER 4
ABOUT THE DAY OF THE FUNERAL

June 25, 2021

I'm not sure how to do today.

I'm not sure why I have to do the things we will be doing today.

I'm not sure why it seems that my blessings were stripped from me.

I'm not sure why my boys have to grow up without their mommy by their side.

I'm not sure how strong that I can be.

I'm not sure when my brain, my heart, and my actions will all line back in sync with each other.

I'm not sure if that makes sense.

I'm not sure of the purpose in all of this; how does this work for good?

I'm not sure I will have answers for the boys when they ask where Mommy is.

I'm not sure they'd understand when I tell them where Mommy is.

But . . .

I am sure in the One that Carol served.

I am sure that God has never left our side.

I am sure that Carol is by His side.

I am sure that we will again be reunited.

I am sure that Carol no longer deals with anxiety.

I am sure that Carol has realized the magnitude of the glory of God.

I am sure that she would want people to know Christ; we have the fruit of her dedication to the Lord all around us.

I am sure that God is still good and faithful.

I am sure that I may temporarily forget that in moments of grief and pain, but it doesn't change the truth that God is near.

I am sure of how big our God is.

I am sure that I will make it through this as I have in many tough times, but it is so hard without my encouraging wife walking in step with me.

I am reminded of many times throughout Scripture when God exercises His greatness—not the times with His power, might, and miracles but this time with the greatness of His Words that simply allow us a glimpse into His being.

"I am."

"I am" is how God responds to Moses. I am who I am. I am the I am. I am that I am. I am.

Jesus responds as well with his own "I am" statements. I am the bread of life, I am the gate, I am the good shepherd, I am the light of the world, I am the vine, I am the way, the truth, and the life, I am the resurrection and the life.

Sometimes words just seem to be words but not when they are spoken by God.

The last words that I was able to speak to Carol were along the lines of "Have fun. I love you. I'll see you later."

I will see her later.

It's hard to be sure of many things in this fading world. I'm thankful that this world is not where our hope rests.

I am sure of where Carol is because she knew the "I AM."

I am not sure why she is gone, but that is OK because I am sure of the "I AM."[3]

I was in full-time church ministry for nearly twenty years. I've preached at many funerals, worked sound at many funerals, and have attended many funerals; however, nothing could have prepared me for my own wife's funeral. I remember in detail many aspects of Carol's funeral. The mental picture that I took as I stood in the back of the large church auditorium has been permanently burned into my memory bank. The lights from the stage behind my wife's lavender casket reflected off of it, and the flowers, vases, and flower towers lined up from one end of the stage to the other flanked both sides of my bride. A slide-show of pictures of Carol from throughout her life played in the background. The songs that we chose, the minister preaching up on stage slightly behind her where she lay—it's all fresh in my mind. I remember the words that her father spoke as he remembered his daughter. I remember her brother pleading with those in attendance to know who Christ is just as Carol knew Him. I remember reading from her Scripture journal. I remember the tornado sirens blaring outside, warning us of danger. I remember my son alone in front of the casket staring at his mother. I remember it all.

Carol passed on a Friday night, and it was the following Friday that we had her funeral. It was the longest week of my life, and yet I didn't want it to end. I didn't want that finality of her being gone. It's not uncommon to have delays between the time of death and the funeral nowadays. We knew that there were going to be many people attending the funeral, and we wanted to be sure each person had the opportunity. Having the funeral on a Friday afternoon allowed us to let people who were very special to myself and Carol come and see her one last time and take part in the funeral.

I spent most of the week leading up to the funeral in my bedroom. I would go through pictures. I would cry. I would ask God why. I would look at more pictures. I would cry some more. When I wasn't doing those things, I would go and see the boys, who were just outside that bedroom door with my family, or I would go for a walk. We actually had a week of camp going on at the property, so there were times that I would go make sure the camp was running smoothly. They didn't need me to do that. I needed that though.

I also had to prepare for the funeral. I never would have imagined what all a person goes through in planning a funeral and the emotions that encircle you like a swarm of vultures waiting for you to lie down and give up.

The day of the funeral was hard. I didn't know how to do it. I didn't want to put on an "I'm OK" face. I didn't want to face that day, let alone face everyone else. I needed it though. I needed the closure that the celebration of life brings. That's what it was—a celebration of Carol's life. It was a funeral, but it was so much more than that as we focused on Carol's acceptance of Christ as the leader of her life. It was not a day that will live in sadness but a day that we remembered her as the follower of Christ that she was.

There are a few things about that day that I remember very specifically and vividly, as I mentioned earlier.

My Nine-Year-Old Son

I allowed my oldest son to be a part of the funeral as he was nine years old at the time and understood what was happening. My two younger boys, one and three years old at the time, were in the nursery during the funeral. I wasn't sure of proper funeral etiquette for very young children when the funeral is for their mother. I was afraid that they would see Mommy lying there, but Mommy wouldn't get up to play with them and they would make a big scene. I would have been broken for good if that were to happen. I elected to have them in the nursery after someone volunteered to watch them for me.

One of the images in my head that I don't believe will ever leave me is when I saw my son staring at his mother lying there in her casket. That broke me. It still breaks me. I can't imagine the thoughts, emotions, and questions that were rolling through his mind at that time. He just stood there with his hands in his pockets looking at his mommy. People would go over to him, myself included, and comfort him and have him go and see a family member, but not too long after that he would be back at his mother's side. Just as I didn't know how to tell him that his mother had died, I didn't know how to take him away from his mother.

I still don't know if I did things correctly. I was just there for him. We were just there for him. I didn't make him talk, but I also didn't let him sit alone. I allowed him to sit quietly, cry, or talk but not be completely alone. I instructed family to not say anything but to just sit with him unless he asked a question.

The Tornado Sirens

I still don't know if there was an actual tornado within twenty miles of us, but the sirens started blaring about three-quarters of the way through the sermon. It was easy to tell who had forgotten to turn their phones to silent as many phones went off at the same time, warning us of a potential tornado and calling all to take shelter. I was in the front row, so I was unsure of what was happening behind me until after the funeral, but I knew that my sister had been tracking the storm with her phone in the row behind me and she hadn't gone to take cover, so I figured everything was all right.

After the minister had finished preaching, he took his place at the head of the casket as those in attendance were guided to walk by Carol and to have a final viewing and say a final good-bye. I walked up to him and let him know that we were under a tornado warning and that the sirens were going off. He had no idea, but from what I was told later, it doesn't surprise me that he didn't know something was going on. Not one person in attendance did anything out of the ordinary when the sirens and warning went off. Not one person got up, nor did anyone have their head buried in their phone. The minister had no idea something was going on because everything looked as it should.

I was told by my cousin, who was standing in the back of the auditorium at the time of the tornado warning, that it was a testament to how many cared for Carol and our family because not one person got up or moved. Granted, we live in the Midwest and a tornado siren may be an invitation for us to go outside and look, but in this moment, not one person moved or left to take shelter. Whether that was irresponsible or just great faith, it meant a lot to me. We felt blessed to see so many people there and that they were there no matter what.

The Prayer Journal
At the funeral we allowed family members, if they desired, to say a few words that had been written ahead of time. It's hard to put into words what you want to say as your final words in honor of and to your loved one. Carol's brother and father both were

able to find some words and speak at the funeral. My mother wrote a letter and had the minister read it.

I couldn't find those words for myself. I did find Carol's words though.

I wanted her words to be a testament of her faith and growth through Christ. Carol dealt with anxiety her entire life, but through Christ and her commitment to Scripture, surrounding herself with the body of Christ and intentionally using her talents to bring glory to God, she found herself capable of doing things that she never thought she could.

My wife did a lot of Bible studies. She loved art journaling, Scripture journaling, and prayer journaling. I found all of these during that first week without her by my side. It has kept a part of her alive. To this day, I can open these journals and read these things and be comforted by her faith and commitment.

The minister offered to read these prayers for me, but I wanted to do that on my own. Now, whether anyone could understand me as I read them through the crying and the huge lump in my throat is a different story. So, here they are without me trying to read them through tears.

Lord, you are so awesome! Every day I learn more of you, and I grow more in love with you. I thank you for the church. Having other believers who care about me and encourage me is a gift. I especially thank you for bringing us to BCC! The people here are great examples of what the church is supposed to look like. I pray that BCC continues to grow in you. I want to see everyone use their gifts from you to glorify you so that those who don't believe yet will come to you. I pray that we always look to your Word for guidance so that we don't get caught up in the trickery of men and false doctrine.

I pray the church speaks only the truth!

I pray that I remember to encourage those in the church. I also want you to use me in your church. Help me to learn of my gifts and talents and how you want me to use them. I pray for courage to use my gifts for you and that I always remember who they are from. I want the focus to always be on you! Amen.

Lord, I know you want to use me to encourage others who may have some of the same struggles as me. Help me to recognize the times in my life that you carried me through. Help me to sort out my testimony so I use my story to help and encourage others. Give me opportunities to share it with others. Give me courage to be able to share my story.

I always felt a little different from everyone else growing up. I knew my anxiety wasn't "normal," but I knew nothing different. I can see how you have always been there during anxiety and panic episodes. You have also given me a passion for creativity. I know this gift of creativity was to help me cope, but I am now seeing that you want me to use it to build up the church and to be an encouragement.

I pray that you give me the skills to create beautiful things and that I am always growing in my creativity. Give me opportunities to use art to show others your love.

I pray that I never use my talents to glorify myself. I am nothing without you. Keep my focus on you only! Amen!

I fully believe that while Carol had opportunities to share her faith while on this earth, just as she prayed for, God has given me opportunities to share of Carol's faith even while she is no longer here. I pray her legacy of service and love live on through myself, our boys, and all those she impacted. May all the glory go to God!

The Graveside Service

It was pouring, and it was a cold rain.

People were committed to being there for us though. I felt bad as I was dry under the tent while others were standing in the pouring rain. I know they couldn't hear any words or the prayer, but I don't think that mattered to them. They stood there, paying their respects as their nice shoes, suits, and dresses were completely soaked. Many of them had to travel a few hours back home as people showed up from every place that we had ever served in ministry.

We are so thankful for those friends and family who showed up for us, getting wet and maybe ruining their clothes at the graveside service.

The Cemetery

I guess I'm fortunate that I live just minutes from the cemetery and can visit often. In the beginning, I visited the cemetery daily. I don't know what is normal, but I'm sure that everyone's normal is different. I visit Carol often still to this day, although my guess is that those visits will eventually become more planned and move to more of a scheduled thing.

The day after she was laid to rest, I made a visit to her gravesite to find that there was a simple metal sign that had her name and her dates on it, as well as a large flower display. I placed flowers there next to the sign and knelt down, forgetting that the ground was sopping wet. I didn't care. I was a mess in every other way, what was a little water and mud?

I've tried searching what other people do when they visit graves of loved ones, and I don't think there is one way to visit your lost loved ones. It's all a part of the grieving process, and how we make it through that process is going to look different for each person.

My visits often start out talking to Carol. I tell her about the boys and what they are doing, I tell her what I've been up to, and I update her on her parents. I tell her of things that I have struggled with and have learned since she has been gone. I tell her about things that are coming up for the boys and me.

Most of the time I start talking to her but end up talking to God. While I wish that I could speak to Carol and she would hear me, it is my opinion that it isn't possible. However, I can talk to God and know that He hears me. So, my speaking at Carol's grave starts as me talking to Carol but transitions to me speaking to God.

I don't leave that grave with peace if I haven't had communion with God first. I'm not talking about bringing grape juice and bread to the cemetery but about having one-on-one fellowship with God. We should be doing that daily, but if I don't speak to God there at the grave when I am sad, then I find myself leaving there feeling incomplete. I need that communion time with God.

I find it helpful that the cemetery is in a beautiful, rural location. Carol and I both loved rural areas, and I've found that it's easier to breathe, think, and be less distracted in that setting.

If you look out to the west of the cemetery, you will see a farm. Often you can see the cows off in the pasture. There is a barn just to the northwest, and the farmhouse is near it. I like to visit at sunset. Carol and I loved viewing sunsets together. She would have loved the sunsets out there, the sun setting over the farmland as you stand and see her headstone.

I picked out a dark, granite headstone with a smooth top and sides for a clean look, and it sits on a base of granite with textured sides. The reasoning for having a base with textured sides is for landscaping purposes. Her headstone has white letters with her name and dates etched on it. Above her name is a flower, the closest design that I could find that resembled a sunflower, because she loved sunflowers. There is a picture of a butterfly flying next to the flower. On the back of the headstone, it says "Loving wife" with a white heart etched just below it. "Mother of" is below the heart with our three boys' names. "Beloved daughter and sister" is at the bottom of the headstone, remembering her parents and brother.

Reflection: The Emotional Roller Coaster

What a whirlwind of emotions those who are grieving go through! It truly is a roller coaster. Up and down with a curve here and there, then a couple of loop the loops and the ride is over . . . but it isn't. That's just one day, right? That is what that funeral day and each day following it felt like for me for quite a while. At Worlds of Fun Theme Park in Kansas City, Missouri, there is a wooden roller coaster called Timber Wolf. Before the

Timber Wolf went through a retracking construction to make it a smoother ride, it felt like going to a chiropractor appointment performed by a stampede of rhinos. It would go up and down and side to side and throw you one way to the next. Don't get me wrong; this was awesome when I was a teenager! It was a matter of pride that you liked riding the Timber Wolf roller coaster. The thrill of going fast was tag-teamed with the fear of what was just around the corner. The direction we would be tossed was easy to figure out the first time but just as painful every time. It was a lot happening all at once, but the ride eventually came to an end. Grief takes the same track except with sadness and despair. There is no thrill.

What feels like a never-ending roller coaster will come to a stop. There will be a time that the ride levels out, the speed slows down, and the tossing back and forth eases up. The immediate decisions of what to do will be made, and a time of healing can begin. This isn't a ride that we'd get back in line for, but it is a ride that we can reflect and learn from being on. We can grow along the ride. I hope you do grow through this. I pray that you strap in and hold on while taking the curves and the ups and downs along the way. May you be strong when you have to be and vulnerable when you need to be. You can make it through this ride!

I lift up my eyes to the mountains—
    where does my help come from?
My help comes from the LORD,
    the Maker of heaven and earth.

—Psalm 121:1–2

CHAPTER 5
ABOUT THOSE TOUGH DECISIONS

This is a tricky chapter to write because it involves tough decisions that you may currently be making for your loved one, ahead of your loved one's passing, or in advance of your own funeral and burial. I will write it just as I handled it. I'm not sure that there is an exact science for making plans in the immediate aftermath of loss or even in advance. Either way, I hope that as you read how I learned through the process, it may save you and others from having to make some of those choices blindly in times of grief. If you are in that time of grief right now, I hope that you can use this chapter to help face some of the tough decisions or at least be prepared to answer some of these questions. Most of these arrangements are good to have prepared prior to someone's death. Making these choices in advance allows those who are grieving the opportunity to do so without having to make tough decisions on top of grief.

All decisions feel like they carry such weight when you're unprepared. Can you ever be fully prepared for the loss of a loved one? I don't think you can, but I do pray that this simple list of things to know might help you in your time of loss and decision-making.

Funeral Home Choice

This was actually the first decision that I had to make when planning for Carol's funeral. In fact, I had to decide in the hospital room on the very night that she passed. Had my parents not been there with me, I don't know what I would've done. We chose the right funeral home. They were wonderful to us. I can't speak highly enough of how they treated me and Carol. They were for us each step of the way.

The hospital has to know which funeral home to call in order to transfer your loved one from the hospital to their facilities to care for them and prepare them for the funeral. The funeral home will ask you questions like these:

- Will you be choosing cremation or burial?
- If cremation, what urn would you like?
- If burial, open casket or closed casket?
- If burial, what casket would you like?
- If burial, what casket vault would you like?
- Do you have an obituary?
- Do you want the obituary to be only online or also in the newspaper?
- Do you have a photograph of your loved one to go along with the obituary?
- Is the funeral to be at a church or at the funeral home?
- Would you like us to prepare and print bulletins for the funeral?
- Do you have a slideshow of pictures?
- Will you have pallbearers?
- Where will your loved one be laid to rest? Which cemetery?

- Do you have a burial plot already?
- Is there going to be a graveside service?
- Would you like a family car to the cemetery?
- Is there an "in memory of" donation request or "in memorial" fund?
- Will you want a large bouquet of flowers on the casket?
- What kind of flowers?
- Which florist will you get the flowers from?
- What would you like your loved one to wear in the casket?
- Do you want your loved one to have jewelry, glasses, rings, etc.?
- Do you have a recent picture of your loved one so that hair and makeup can be as close as possible to normal?
- How many death certificates do you need? *(In the event an autopsy is performed, as we had, it may take longer to get those death certificates to you.)*
- Will there be a visitation? When will that take place?
- Will you be ordering a headstone or a flat grave marker? *(Some cemeteries have rules against upright headstones.)*
- What color will the headstone be? Will it have a vase or no vase? Rough edges or smooth? White letters?

Funeral Order of Service

The order of service that we had for my wife was pretty standard. Do you desire a faith-based service for your loved one? Do you want an open mic part of the service? Would you like specific songs to be played, poems or scriptures to be read? I've given you what I decided when it came to the funeral, but there can be all different types of funerals. The question that drove most of my decisions was this: "What best displays who Carol was?" I made each decision by asking that question first.

Final Moments Together with Your Loved One

I cleared the room of every guest, acquaintance, and even family member when it came time to say a final goodbye to my Carol. Everyone else had gone through the line to give their final respects and to see Carol for the last time except for me. I asked the funeral directors to clear the room and provide me the space to see her one final time. When so many people are around you on such a busy day, it can get overwhelming. I just needed a space that had no talking, no music, no distractions, a space that just had Carol and me in it. I had to say goodbye, and I got to say that final goodbye on my own terms. It wasn't the hospital calling me to get there because she was coding. It wasn't the doctor calling to tell me that she was gone when I was so close to seeing her. It wasn't an unexpected moment for my final goodbye but one that I was able to have with her at my own choosing. I'm so glad now that I took that time to clear the room for the two of us. I didn't know that I needed that until later on; at that time, it was just me getting rid of the noise around me. While I knew that she was gone and it was just her body in front of me, I said goodbye and was able to do so without the noise or presence of people watching me.

Casket Picking

My mother-in-law, Wanda, is the one who picked the casket. My in-laws actually came to me and said that they were going to pay for the funeral and all of its expenses. That was such a blessing! When it came to picking the casket and casket vault, I gave them the driver's seat. We looked at a couple but then came up to this really pretty purple casket. It was the one. Wanda knew it immediately, and if you've read the chapter "About the Day of the Funeral," you know that it was a beautiful service, and the purple, which was Carol's favorite color, was a wonderful pick.

The vault was just a vault. They all were the same color. My in-laws picked it out as well. Not that it was a hard decision to pick the vault that the casket rests in, but any decision among the million tiny decisions that needed to be made felt hard. I didn't even know that you had to purchase the vault. It makes absolute sense to me now, but this is one of the many things that I didn't know before this tragedy.

Cemetery and Funeral Plot

Many of my relatives on my father's side of the family are buried in the same small-town cemetery. In fact, at this time my uncle is the caretaker of the cemetery. That's where Carol was laid to rest as well. She is buried among other members of the immediate and extended Tyler family. She is near my sister who died in 2006. She is close to my grandparents, Wilson and Ruth Tyler. She lies near my aunt Joyce. One day, she'll lie beside my parents and many others of my extended family. I also have a plot right next to hers.

My family came to my side and took care of Carol's burial plot. It's an expense that I had never thought about until I had to think about it. For some, it may not make a difference where they are buried. Some may choose to be cremated and continue to reside next to their living loved ones or have their ashes spread over a favorite place.

Again, the question "What best displays who Carol was?" led each decision I made. My wife was a close-knit person when it came to family and friends. It only felt right to put her near family and near us. No matter where life takes the boys and me in the future, we'll always come home for visits, and she has been laid to rest at home. Carol's parents also have decided that they'd like to be buried at that same cemetery. It's just a small-town cemetery, but it's peaceful!

Single or Double Headstone

I believe that for those who are married and whose spouse dies young, this may be the hardest decision to make. The worst, most awful, sleep-depriving decision that I had to make was if I was going to get a single or double headstone. It sounds silly because no one else put any pressure on the decision or would have thought twice about if I chose single or double, but I fretted over making this decision. I was so nervous about it. I wanted to put it off until another day. I sought advice and still felt lost.

I loathed this decision that I had to make.

I am not exaggerating when I say that I lost sleep over this decision. My thought process was that if I got a double head-stone, then I would see my name up there each time that I went to visit Carol's grave. I also know that while I am not a young kid any longer, I may still have many years ahead of me. I am forever tied to Carol and our lives are forever connected, yet life continues to move forward on this earth for the living. There may come a day that God makes it known that my story still has companionship in it. I thought that having a double headstone could be weird and awkward for me and maybe for my future. On the other side of things, my thought process had me think-ing that a single headstone would have only her name on it, that my love for her wasn't deep enough to get a double headstone, that I was betraying her and her memory. I worried that if I chose a single headstone that everyone would question why I didn't get a double headstone. I didn't want her family to think that I didn't care for her. I also didn't want to realize my mortality at each visit to Carol's gravesite. (Now, the reality of life and death is very real, and it's easier, in my opinion, to think of what comes after our lives are done on earth when your spouse is no longer with you.) I continued to go back and forth on the decision. It was eventually decided after I texted Carol's mother.

I texted Wanda and told her that I was struggling with that decision and explained why. She said that she fully understood and that she and Kevin had talked through what the future may hold for both of our families. She assured me that they were fully behind any decision that I made. I was so thankful for that. They truly are and will forever be my family as well.

I ended up getting a single headstone, and it is fully dedicated to Carol, and it is perfect. I'm thankful for the decision and the support that I was given in making it, and in all reality, whatever my future holds, the headstone is a piece of rock that can be changed and replaced as long as the money is there to pay for it.

What to Write on the Headstone or Grave Marker

I've read of people's famous last words. Some of them are funny, lighthearted, and silly, while some are tragic and terrifying. The basic function of a headstone is to let everyone know who rests in that spot. A grave marker doesn't have to be a grand gesture, wordy, or inspirational. Most times, simplicity goes further and looks cleaner. Some put scripture on headstones. Others may have a picture etched into stone of their loved one. The typical headstone, or grave marker, will have the person's full name, birth date, and death date. How much you can put on a headstone or marker depends on how much space it has. As you read in the previous chapter, we had a flower and butterfly etched into Carol's headstone on the front side. You can use both sides of a headstone and put more information on the other side. In my personal opinion, when in doubt, keep it simple. In many cemeteries, you can decorate around the headstone with flowers, flags, or pictures. You will be visiting your loved one, and the marker will be at that spot when you visit.

Death Certificates

Everyone wants a death certificate. This is not something that I would've ever thought that I would need to think about. I figured that they'd give you a death certificate, and you could make copies as needed. That's not the case. I had a friend walk through this process with me, and one thing he mentioned before we ever went to the funeral home was to think about how many death certificates that I would need. Credit card companies, the Social Security office, life insurance agencies, banks, and student loan companies—they all want an official, "original" version, not a copy. I also didn't realize that death certificates cost money.

The funeral director is usually the person who files your loved one's information with the state's office of vital records. As such, he or she will also request at that time the number of death certificates you will need. Because each copy that is provided by the office of vital records is considered an official, "original" document, not a copy, it will cost a fee. Those fees vary from state to state and may be cheaper if requested all at one time, but your funeral director will be able to tell you the details.

Obituary

I didn't write the obituary. Actually, no one related to Carol wrote her obituary. A friend of ours wrote it for us. Our friend sat with me and kind of formed it just in talking with me and then also with Carol's family. Then, when he had that information gathered up, he wrote it for us. I think I had him change one thing when he gave me what he had written.

Some funeral homes have an obituary template, but if they don't and you are wondering what should go in an obituary, the answer is simple: whatever you would like. As you can probably guess, I asked myself what would best show who Carol was, so here's what I included:

- brief description of childhood: date of birth, birth location, high school graduation date, and name of high school
- description of young adulthood: further education location, date of graduation, etc.
- marriage: brief history of how we met, date of marriage
- kids: names and ages
- work/ministry history *(It was important for us to include this as she was a servant at heart.)*
- hobbies: sports, baking, painting, etc.
- date of death and location
- "preceded in death by" section with names of family members
- "survived by" section is often included for living family members
- funeral location, times of services, officiating minister's name, pallbearers' names
- "in memorial" or "in memory of" information

Where to Have the Funeral

Most funeral homes will allow you to have the funeral at their location. They hold visitations and usually have a small chapel on site for the funeral. Generally, if you are a part of a church or a family member is part of a church, that church will allow you to have a funeral at their location. Members of churches will probably have no charge involved for use of the building, and a dinner might even be provided for the family. That is generally the case. There may be a charge for using a church building if you or your loved one is not a member. This covers cleaning fees, sound equipment use, and their time. Believe me when I say that most churches are not out to get your money but are out to help you in your time of need. Call on your local church in your time of need.

Graveside Service

A graveside service is generally very short. If a graveside service takes the place of a traditional funeral, then it may take longer. Most graveside services that I've been a part of had the family seated next to the casket, which lies above the burial plot, and a small service. The minister, or officiant, will usually recite a scripture or short devotion. In some services, balloons or lanterns are released, or there is some other visible example of letting the loved one go or expression of love for the deceased. If the person was a veteran and/or in good standing with the military, a gun salute can take place at the graveside. That is something neat to experience.

Who Should Speak at the Funeral

I've spoken already about Carol's funeral and how we had four speakers. When it comes to funeral speakers, the fewer, the better. That comes with an exception, however. If each speaker is going to share a prepared speech, then more is OK. Often, the minister, or officiant, is joined by a loved one to read a poem or sing a song, but I've been to funerals where there is an unscripted, open mic opportunity for all in attendance. That could be wonderful and what you want, but I've seen it turn ugly. I've heard some people bash others, mutual friends of the deceased, and then talk themselves up in the same breath. I've seen people get critical of the deceased and their life choices. I've also seen and heard someone tell a story from the microphone that had nothing to do with the deceased.

If at all possible, keep the speeches scripted and have all speakers write out in advance what they plan to share. You'll look back on it and thank yourself; people will thank you if you are preparing for your own funeral. People tend to write out their thoughts better than they speak them while experiencing a whirl of emotions in front of people.

Wedding Rings

I debated on what to do when it came to Carol's wedding rings. This was a decision that I made in the hospital room that night right before we had to leave. It was not a decision that I had to make at that time, but I didn't know that it could wait. This was all new territory for me, and I'm not sure anyone really knows right from wrong in those moments. Before I left the hospital, I asked the nurse to go back in and retrieve Carol's rings for me. My thinking was that Blake might want them some day for his bride. The week leading up to the funeral, I went out and bought her a silver ring that was very close in likeness to place on her hand for the rest of time.

It wasn't just her rings that I was conflicted about. How long do I wear my wedding ring? Is there an appropriate amount of time for a widow or widower to wear their ring? I tried wearing it. I wore it on my left hand as normal, then I moved it to the right hand, but nothing felt right. I tried going without it but then felt I was betraying my commitment. It wasn't until I put the rings together that I was OK not wearing that symbol of commitment to Carol. They are together as they were meant to be. It felt right.

What to Do with All Their Stuff

After Carol passed away, I started typing into search engines "What do I do now after my loved one died?" I would scroll the many, many opinions and articles online about being a widower and wonder still what I was supposed to do. I remember reading to not make any big decisions for six months and to just grieve. Another source said to wait one or two years before making any large decisions. Pick a number of years to wait for making any choice and I'm sure you'll find that advice out there. To be honest, everything felt like a big, important matter at the time. Where do you draw the line? So, I didn't make any decisions that amounted to much. I solved problems as they came but didn't go out trying to fix world hunger.

A couple of months before Carol's passing, we had purchased a pull-behind camper. We were going to use it that summer for a living space for our summer nanny while we had camps in session and then take some family trips in it once our camp season was over and we could get away. Carol was so excited about that camper. We all were. Carol thought, *Oh, the places we can go*, and I thought, *Oh, the money we will save*. She cleaned the camper up and made it cozy and comfy for our summer nanny. Shortly after, Carol passed.

For six months I looked at that camper sitting behind our house. It was still decorated just as she had left it. I went back and forth in my head about whether I wanted to keep the camper. I did want to keep it. I didn't want to keep it. I did; I didn't. Then, one day I realized that I wasn't going to be able to take a trip with my boys in that camper. That camper was for the dream Carol and I had to go and travel together. Although I still found joy in the midst of trial, I was sad that we would not get to use it together. Six months after losing Carol, I sold the camper, and it felt right. I had peace with that decision.

It's funny to me that some of the things that I thought I used to treasure are the things that I'd ditch first in a fire. The things now that I treasure most are the things I would've never thought about. I keep all her journals in one place. I have all our pictures ready to be picked up quickly if we ever need to evacuate. One of her journals I keep in a fireproof safe with other "valuables." The camper was just a something. Vehicles are just somethings. Video game consoles, TVs, computers—all just somethings. I want to keep the things that bring me joy. Carol's journals, artwork, and our pictures—those things bring me joy. The rest is just stuff.

I heard about a guy who didn't want to get rid of his wife's stuff after she had passed, and I can relate. What he did with his wife's things is something I would have never thought to do. He rented a temperature-controlled storage unit and put all her stuff in there. It was nice and organized, and he was going to keep it that way until he felt that he could part with her things. I don't know if that time ever came or if that stuff is in that storage unit to this day. I hear of others who don't touch anything in the house that their loved one may have touched or used regularly. I've also heard of people who dumped everything that had belonged to their loved one and then regretted that decision some time down the road. You've probably figured out that I am a thinker before I am a doer. Don't misunderstand; I go all in and do things without thinking sometimes, but on big decisions, I think a lot, in hopes that I make the right decision.

The idea is that we take our time in making those big decisions and learn how to let go of things. We will find that some things that initially only brought us sadness and a realization of what was lost bring us comfort later. I still have my wife's clothes hanging in the closet. I still have the fake sunflowers over the kitchen windows that she placed there. I still have most of her craft things, artwork, and crafting tools. The fake spinning wheel that she bought at an auction or garage sale still sits outside my house for decoration. I still have all those things, but I know that many of those things are just things and will be donated or handed out to family. I realize now, though, that I will treasure her notes and letters to me more than I ever will treasure her tennis shoes hanging on the closet door. I know now that our pictures together will bring me more joy than a fake sunflower above a window.

Carol loved to wear cardigans. She had this yellow cardigan that she especially loved. I mean, if she could have worn it every day, she would have. To be honest, she bought a second yellow cardigan similar to her favorite one so that she'd have two and then we couldn't tease her about never changing her clothes. One way that it has been easier to work through the thoughts of donating or parting with her clothing is that I went through and picked out the clothing that she wore regularly. A family member offered to take some of her clothing and have it turned into stuffed bears and pillows for us to have. It's seriously a cool idea and something that my oldest son has really appreciated. I kept her favorite Charlie Brown hoodie but gave her aunt Jackie that bag of regularly used clothing, not knowing what we would be getting back in return. One of those clothing items was that darn yellow cardigan. It's neat, though, because now we have a yellow-cardigan pillow and a yellow-cardigan stuffed bear. We, my son Blake and I, were looking through the pillows and bears when we got them back, knowing that her family was going to pick some, and Blake immediately said, "Don't give away the yellow ones." He finds memories and comfort in those things as well. It's something of his mother's possessions, and he doesn't want to part with them either.

If I were pressed to give advice on what to do or when is it time to part with your loved one's things, I'd say that I wouldn't narrow it down to a certain number of days or months or years before you make any decisions. Some decisions are going to be right there in front of you when it comes to how you do life in the immediate aftermath of loss. A one-week decision that I needed to make was what I was going to do with the boys during the day now that Carol wasn't there to stay at home with them. I had to decide that quickly, and they began going to day care for the first time ever in their lives. On the other hand, I could wait six months before I sold the camper. My advice would be to take your time on decisions that don't have to be made right now, and know that in time you will begin to heal, and you will then know what to keep and what to part with. Work through those decisions, and if you don't have peace either way, then it's probably not time.

I get it. It's hard to deal with the physical items that our loved ones have left behind. I'm not an advocate of getting rid of all their stuff, but I'm also not an advocate of keeping all their stuff. Take your time to find which of their possessions brings you joy. It may be just a few items. Seeing their things left behind is hard. Make decisions when you have to, and take your time with the decisions that are not urgent. You can do this.

Reflection: The Coat of Many Colors

I've always wondered what Jacob of the Bible did with his son Joseph's coat of many colors when it was returned to him. In Genesis 37, we read the account of Jacob and his sons. Jacob favored his son Joseph as he was born to him in his old age. He gave Joseph a special coat, known as the coat of many colors. Joseph's brothers despised him because of it. While in the fields, they saw an opportunity to be rid of Joseph and took it. They sold Joseph into slavery and then took his coat covered in goat blood back to their father, saying that Joseph had been killed. Jacob entered a time of mourning and refused to be comforted. He sought out to mourn until the end of his days.

Did he trash the ornate coat? Did he keep it? Did they split up Joseph's things? Did they have a burial without the body? We don't know the answers to those questions, but it is a perfect example of decisions that many before us have had to ponder as well. Find comfort knowing that you are not the first to make these tough choices. May you have clarity as you make decisions. May you find support in the community around you. Let discernment and grace be given to you in great amounts. May you find peace in the decisions that you make.

Blessed are the poor in spirit,
    for theirs is the kingdom of heaven.
Blessed are those who mourn,
    for they will be comforted.

—Matthew 5:3–4

CHAPTER 6
ABOUT THE EMPTINESS

The hardest thing to do initially once Carol passed was to go anywhere on my own. It wasn't that I couldn't go on my own or wasn't willing to, but going by myself somewhere meant that there'd be an empty seat next to or across from me.

Some of you lost your spouses after many, many more years of marriage than Carol and I were together. But for fourteen years, I didn't have an empty seat next to or across from me. Carol always filled it. She was always there. She was a constant. Whether we were on the couch watching TV, sitting in a coffee shop, dining at a restaurant or with family and friends, there she was. Now she is not.

August 9, 2021

Today would have been our thirteenth anniversary.

It's such a strange feeling, for lack of better words, to have this day of what would have been celebration and then to be alone for it.

Many didn't know that it was today. Most of who I talked to today, in person or via other ways, wouldn't have had any idea. I stayed to myself mostly, aside from some texts, snaps, and a phone call or two. It's a weird thing to bring up in conversation, and something I wouldn't have done anyway.

The hardest part of today for me was eating lunch. I went to Firehouse Subs, and I sat outside, and in the middle of eating, even though I knew I was by myself, I noticed the empty chair across from me.

That single empty chair.

That was the hardest part of the day.

It wasn't waking up early to give the boys baths and making sure everyone got to day care and school. It wasn't visiting Carol's gravesite, it wasn't washing and cleaning the vehicle, it wasn't picking the boys up, nor was it grocery shopping with all three of them. It wasn't bedtime or helping Blake with homework.

It was looking at an empty chair.

That empty chair . . . it got me.

Thankfully it was ninety degrees outside and I was sweating, so any tears sliding down my face looked like sweat.

I'm thankful for the almost thirteen years to have been married to Carol. Never would I have imagined that I would be without her. It's a whole new way of life now. Not one thing is the same. My thinking has changed. My mindset has changed. My intentionality has changed. My outlook on the future, tomorrow and today—it's all changed.

Some of you said, "You're doing such a great job" or "You are a great dad." I appreciate that from the bottom of my heart. I am not doing and sharing our lives to prove that I can or that we are all right—I just want to be a dad that is present in the moment with my boys.

I am constantly reminded (daily, hourly) that tomorrow is not promised, and I want my boys, my family, and my friends to know that they matter to me. I may be more tired, but chances are high that we'll take that extra trip to the park to play. Putting things off until tomorrow, unless it's dishes or laundry, is no longer what I want. If I'm honest, I didn't want to go through the Mark Twain Cave on vacation with all three of the boys. I tried talking myself out of it. I'm glad I didn't find an excuse. I'm glad I sucked it up and did it. Not for the accolades but because of the boys. Someone commented something to the extent on one of my posts, "It's good for the boys to see Daddy continue to live."

That's what I want.

I want Blake to know that it's OK to be sad, but it's also OK to live a full life. I want the littles to know who Carol was and how much she loved them. I also want them to experience a life of love, and I can't offer that to them if I refuse to "continue to live."

How easy it would be to sit inside the house and do nothing. How easy it could be to sink into depression. How easy it could be to neglect reality and "live" in sadness.

I refuse to live in sadness. I refuse to live in bitterness. I refuse to live in anger. I refuse to live in the "what-ifs."

I choose to live life. I choose to find joy. I choose to find happiness. I choose to make new friends and dig deeper with old friendships. I choose to be intentional. I choose to let you know that you matter to me.[4]

The Loneliness

Loneliness is debilitating. Loneliness can lead to bad decisions. Loneliness is not the same as aloneness.

Loneliness didn't hit right away for me. I still had this feeling that her absence was temporary, even though I knew in my mind that she was gone forever. It didn't feel real. It hadn't fully taken root in my life that she was never coming back. Even though I knew it in my heart, it didn't feel like the truth. She was just here. I had just talked to her. It wasn't some long sickness that we knew would end in death. It wasn't even a sickness that she was dealing with for any period of time. It was just that she was here when she went to the hospital and then she wasn't.

Our world had shattered, and yet it didn't feel real.

All the responsibilities of two people were still there, yet one of us was gone forever. I went through the motions of being present for a while before I acknowledged that she was gone. I had to accept her absence as being forever. Once I accepted that she was not coming back, I then recognized that I had to be present and not just fake it. I had to be present for the boys. I had to be present for my career. I had to be present for Carol. I had to be present to do my service to the Lord. I had to be present for me.

So, I have learned (and am still learning) how to live in the "alone."

Living in the "alone" was not an easy process to learn because loneliness gripped me. Loneliness creeps in and takes ahold of every part of our lives if we are not careful. I found myself lying on the bed crying for hours when the boys were at school and day care because of the loneliness. I found myself crying as I drove somewhere by myself because of the loneliness. While hanging out with the boys, friends, and family, I was able to be present and have brief periods of respite, but at all other times I was living in loneliness.

Loneliness is defined in many different ways. Loneliness is defined differently by psychologists than it is by mainstream culture. Doctors may define loneliness differently than professors and educators do. The Bible may speak differently about loneliness than all professions do.

However you define it, loneliness is more than just being a little sad and wanting someone to have fun with or celebrate Valentine's Day with. Loneliness for me took shape as crippling bouts of sadness and emptiness. Loneliness lingered because I was constantly reminded that I no longer had my bride to live life with.

I also found loneliness came when I was alone. Imagine that! In those moments when the emotions and clouds of loneliness took over, it confused my perception of living, and it was difficult to see past the hard circumstances. I couldn't focus on work or what I needed to do. When I wasn't present with others, I would take residence in my bed and plead and complain to God that I couldn't do this alone. In those moments, loneliness blinded me to the hope that I had and to the truth that God was still working in my life and still forming the rest of my story.

I felt bad and ashamed for being lonely. I felt bad because in those moments it was as if I was neglecting God's provision and care in my life. It almost felt like a secret sin that I kept going back to. I didn't take on alcohol, drugs, or anything else we view as self-medications for loneliness; loneliness itself is what I allowed to take over my time alone. Loneliness was crippling for me, even though I hid it well. I have tried to be very open with my grief, but no one wants to talk about everything.

I learned that I had to do just that. I had to confront my loneliness. I needed to put God first at all times of my life and not just when I was in public or in view of others. It may sound weird that wallowing in loneliness was my drug of choice, but it was. I mean no offense to those who struggle with, have struggled with, and/or have overcome addictions when it comes to alcohol, drugs, or any other thing that grabs and doesn't let go when I say that loneliness was like that. It was though.

It sounds weird. I know that.

I had to force myself to take the boys to the park in order to not sit at home and put on a TV show or lie in bed. I may have looked like I had it together, but I was struggling to learn this new way of life of single parenting and grieving all in the same moment. I was at the park with my boys to give them something to do but also to keep my mind busy and to see that the world keeps moving. Occasionally, my friends would be able to go to the park as well.

I forced myself to take a vacation with the boys to go see old friends. I remember posting on social media a recap of the vacation as a reminder that we can do hard things. We took a picture after visiting Mark Twain Cave. It was hot, I had the three boys, and I was still learning how to do it all on my own. It's not our best picture, but we did it.

That was a pivotal moment in my learning that I can live in the aloneness rather than being taken over by loneliness when I am alone.

Maybe you're questioning what I view as aloneness. Aloneness to me is acknowledging that I am OK with being alone. It is a season of growth, learning, and leaning into God as the one you depend on. I know that I am not truly *alone* as I serve a God who is always present. I also know that I don't have to have a significant other to be happy or to thrive. Will that be in my future? Maybe. I don't know. God created us to be in community with others, and we are built for relationships. That's a road that I may travel in the future, but my goal is to thrive and grow wherever He has me right now.

I have learned a lot about myself on this journey of grief. I am in this period of the "alone" that is needed to appreciate the blessings that I had, the blessings I have, and the blessings that are still to come. My decisions are clearer now than when I was living in loneliness.

In this season of life, I would be more afraid to live in loneliness than to live in the alone. It's not that I'm embracing the single life as the life to live forever, but I'm letting God have a bigger role in my "alone" rather than forgetting Him in the loneliness. Even when I'm accepting the season of life that I am in, moments present themselves that are difficult to embrace.

The Empty Seats

I opened up this chapter with a social media post that I wrote on what would have been Carol's and my wedding anniversary. As I shared in that post, the concept of the empty seat has been hard for me. There are three other "empty seat" stories that I would like to share with you. In these stories, my father filled the empty seat beside me. Three times he showed up in ways that I never expected but desperately needed. Two of those times, not a word was spoken.

Cafeteria

I mentioned earlier that my family visited in the hospital once there was a complication with Carol's procedure. I had just been able to see her in the ICU and left to let her parents both be able to see her at the same time. I then went and joined my dad, mom, and my older brother, Aaron, in the cafeteria. My brother was trying to lift my spirits. To this point, I hadn't yet cried. The emotions had been boiling up but contained by the adrenaline and constant moving. And then I cried.

I couldn't hold it in any longer. I didn't know what was going on, and, in that moment, it overwhelmed me. So, I cried. I was sitting at the end of a table; my mom and dad were sitting on the left side of me, and my brother was on the right. I don't know if anyone knew how to respond as I cried. How do you respond, really? Even though my wife was still alive, our lives had just changed forever, and everything was going to be different. What was going to happen? Would she be able to recover? Would she need constant care? Had she been without oxygen for too long? Would she wake up? All these questions and possibilities created in me a daze, a confusion, and an overwhelming sadness.

My dad got up from the other side of the table and came over and just stood beside me with his hand on my shoulder. He was just there. He didn't say anything. He was just there, filling the emptiness that I felt at that time.

It was what I needed. I look back and realize I didn't need words. I needed my father standing over me, letting me know that he was there. The parallels to our faith are overwhelming.

The Ride Home

With Carol's rings in a container in my pocket, I picked up the bag that I had prepared for Carol just the night before, and my parents and I headed to the vehicles. They had stayed around to help me with some decisions that had to be made before I left the hospital. As we were heading out, it was decided that I wouldn't be driving home alone. It's not that I wouldn't have been able to, but they believed someone should be with me. My dad is not a city driver, and my mom loves to drive, so we decided that my dad would ride with me in what would have been an empty seat.

On the way home, my father filled the empty passenger seat. I don't know what specifically we talked about, but I know it was about how I didn't understand the whole situation or what had happened. I don't remember a lot of that drive home. I'm glad he rode with me—it distracted me. I needed that distraction because the days ahead were going to be very lonely and the reality of Carol being gone would become all too real.

Church

The day after Carol's death, our minister, Sid, visited. While talking with him, I mentioned that I was going to be at church that next day. We all were. Maybe that isn't a big deal; we go to church every Sunday, but it felt like a big deal at the time. After the conversation with Sid, I was set and determined that the boys and I were going to church that next day.

And we did go to church.

The pain followed.

The awareness and presence of that empty seat next to me was greater than anything in church to me that day. I knew I had made a mistake in coming to church. I couldn't sing the worship songs because I was getting choked up. I couldn't pay attention because I missed my wife. It's like I couldn't worship. I don't remember when exactly it was in the service, but our minister mentioned to the congregation what had happened with Carol.

That was hard.

I couldn't hold back my crying. The tears flowed.

In no time, I felt a hand on my shoulder. My dad had left his seat on one end of the row we were sitting in, went around the church, and came to my side, his hand on my shoulder again, letting me know that I wasn't alone in a room filled with hundreds of people.

My father doesn't know how he helped me in those moments and will never fully realize that impact, but it was huge. To those who are going through the grieving process, embrace those who desire to be at your side. You don't have to talk about your grief, but embrace their desire to walk alongside you.

In your grief, open your eyes to the people who are there with you. Surround yourself with people who will leave their comfort zone to make sure you know that you are not alone. Maybe you already have that person but are blind to it. Open your eyes and look around. That person is there, and if you don't see them, ask God to show you who they are.

Reflection: A Prayer for the Brokenhearted

Father in heaven,

I pray for the one reading. I pray for the brokenhearted. I pray that our emptiness is filled with your fulfilling love. I pray that the void that we feel in our hearts is made complete. May you provide a person or multiple people who are not afraid to sit and listen. May your community, your body of believers, be our community. Thank you for promising to be near to the brokenhearted and those who mourn. Show us how to stay near to you. Provide us wisdom during this difficult time in our lives. Grant us courage when times are troubled. Let us be reminded to seek you always. May your glory be known through our stories. Amen.

So do not fear, for I am with you;
    do not be dismayed, for I am your God.
I will strengthen you and help you;
    I will uphold you with my righteous right hand.

—Isaiah 41:10

CHAPTER 7
ABOUT THE LETTERS AND ACTS OF KINDNESS

I am continually amazed that I still receive letters and cards so long after Carol's death. I attribute that to the amazing person that she was and to the body of Christ that we have been surrounded with and have had the privilege to serve alongside. If I could say one thing about the letters and cards that I received and hope that you all receive in the times of hurting, pain, and grief, it is this: keep them.

Don't toss the cards and letters aside. It is our natural habit to set things aside because we are distracted or feel like they are empty words inside. But, believe me, you'll need them. You read a card or letter in the immediate aftermath of tragedy differently than you do after a period of time has separated you from the tragedy. You hear a different tone in the letter. You read the same words, but their meaning is less "they sent this because they felt obligated to do so" and much more "these words are heartfelt, and they really care for me."

We have received many cards and letters in the mail, and each one means a lot to us. I want to share a few of those letters in this chapter because I believe that you, as the reader, will receive something as well from reading them. I do this with the approval of those who wrote them to us. I hope that by reading these notes you will see that everyone is grieving the same loss but doing so differently. You are not alone! These notes show us all sides of this grief process, and my prayer is that they bless you in your journey of grieving.

I do not share any of these to make myself or Carol sound any better than we are but because they helped pick the boys and me up when we were down. I pray that in your times of grief you, too, will be blessed by the people around you. It is too easy to push them aside. Allow their kind gestures and heartfelt words to help pick you up when you are down. It's not easy for me to read some of the messages that I've received, and tears flowed as I typed them out. Reading the letters, notes, and cards brings back the very raw emotion of losing your loved one, but it's a part of the healing process. While I have included the first names of the people who sent me these notes, I have taken out the more personal parts of their messages to me.

A Letter from Nikki

Seth,

You and your family are constantly in my prayers.

Almost eleven years ago, I walked my sister through the sudden death of her spouse. It shook me to the core. My sister became a widow at the age of thirty-one, left to raise their five-year-old daughter. Those first days of walking through such grief and sadness were so overwhelming for me, but I knew God had put me in my position for "such a time as this."

Grief is such a strange thing. I've heard it said that grief is just another side of love.

"Grief, I've learned, is really just love. It's all the love you want to give, but cannot. All of that unspent love gathers up in the corners of your eyes, the lump in your throat and in that hollow part of your chest. Grief is just love with no place to go." —Jamie Anderson

I had not experienced loss like I had when my brother-in-law died. I had no idea what grief and sadness really were. There were days the weight of grief and sadness was so heavy I could barely get out of bed.

Everyone's grief is so very different, and I've learned that everyone deals with it differently, and that's OK.

I heard a new version of Psalm 23 the other day and wanted to share it with you.

Psalm 23 (NCV)

The LORD is my shepherd;
    I have everything I need.
He lets me rest in green pastures.
    He leads me to calm water.
He gives me **new** strength.
    He leads me on paths that are right
for the good of his name.
    Even if I walk through a very dark valley,
I will not be afraid,
    because you are with me.
Your rod and your shepherd's staff comfort me.

You prepare a meal for me
    in front of my enemies.
You pour oil of blessing on my head;
    you fill my cup to overflowing.
Surely your goodness and love will be with **me**
    all my life,
and I will live in the house of the LORD forever. (emphasis added)

I pray He gives you **new** strength to carry on without Carol and that you see the oil of **blessing** that God has for you and your boys.

Death changed us all, **but** much beauty came from the ashes. Some of the beauty took time to be revealed, **but** I am grateful for the beauty of restored relationships, of cycles of unforgiveness ending, of spiritual growth and maturity in myself and family members, of seeing others come to the Lord, and so much more.[5]

A Letter from Jen

I just wanted to share some things that God has had on my heart since the day that Carol passed away. Your social media post "God is still good. God is still faithful. I don't understand this moment in our lives, but I do know that He does know all things."

I have been a believer my entire life. I come from an extremely strong family of believers. I have suffered losses, a few before their time. I've wrestled with God and come out stronger and unashamed because of it. But I am not writing this to tell you my story.

I realize that there are so many that have at this point sent their hugs, food, condolences, flowers, and anything they can to try to ease the ache. I know you sincerely feel the love of God's people as it surrounds your family and will continue. I wish it were enough.

What I wanted to share with you is something a little different though, and I hope not inappropriate. I hadn't gotten to know Carol, much at all, and I am sad about that, because I believe I have deeply missed out. From all I have heard, she was a quiet, deep thinker, in love with the relationship she had with Jesus that only the two of them could know. She was beginning to understand the magnitude of her gifts and be OK to really sit in them. I believe that what I have to say to you would be something she would love to hear.

Seth, I have never in my life, seen a more tangible display of someone being able to live out their actual belief that "God is still good. God is still faithful" than seeing you in church on Sunday morning, just one full day after Carol went home. **Never**. I have experienced actual miracles on more than one occasion, I have seen unbelievable things in the gifts God has called me to, but to watch you live that out in such absolute boldness was just knee buckling. I realize it wasn't without anguish or even the ability to know how to function or get the boys ready or when to feed everyone that day (including yourself). I know you probably couldn't even open your chest all the way to get a complete breath, and maybe still can't without her. But you showed up in absolute testament of His faithfulness and goodness.

I have had many conversations over that with people since that day. And since that day, you have done it over and over. The grief shows, as it should, you loved her with your entire being. The thing that Carol would be so elated about is that your belief in His faithfulness shows even more. People cannot watch this and not be taken aback in wonder. Even those of us who truly know who He is want to know more of Him that has that kind of power in you.

The testament between you and Carol that has shown itself in this horrific time is the most drawing-to-Jesus thing I have seen in my forty-four years on the planet, even being raised in it. I kid you not, Seth, Carol's life will continue to do amazing things through how you have already handled this.

There is no pressure in that. You grieve her. You fall apart when you need to. Jesus grieved and wept. It shows your incredible love for her. But know this, we all have seen His enormous grace pour over you, and Carol has to be beside herself knowing that her life and even her death has such a stirring of people to need to know the God that is this good and faithful.

I am not even sure if this makes sense, and I sure pray that it does not in any way seem insensitive. I just want you to know that Carol is making such an impact still. And you, my friend, are as well, even in your days that you feel you can barely function. God is showing the rest of us mighty things.[6]

A Note from Dawn

Seth,

Our hearts are breaking for you and the boys. Carol was such a sweetheart! I truly enjoyed our talks and visits. We shared a love for creating things with our hands. She was so talented and would make any crazy thing I would ask of her. Our granddaughters still love the unicorn hat and scarves she made. She always had a smile, even if she didn't feel good. I felt like I could talk to her and she could talk to me. I loved making things for her because she was always so excited about whatever it was—a purple flower or new burp cloths for the babies. It was a joy to know Carol![7]

A Note from Caroline

Seth and boys,

I am so sorry for your loss of Carol. My deepest condolences go to you and your family at this time. I didn't know Carol well, but watching her at a week of camp I saw how wonderful of a person she was. She made all of us feel so loved and cared for at camp. Through her example and actions that week, I saw an amazing example of a follower of Christ, wife, and mother. I hope to be at least half the woman she was. Again, I am so sorry for your loss, and I have been praying for you continually.[8]

A Note from Becky

Dear Seth,

You have been on my mind and heart and in my prayers since the news of Carol. There were so many parallels with your loss events and mine that I grieved all over again . . . the suddenness and unexpectedness is so unnerving. Yet you are helping people in more ways than you know by sharing your grief. Thank you. I encourage you to look for joy in each day and hold on to that for that day, then go to the next. God is growing you, my friend, and you are being refined like gold.[9]

A Note from Sarah

Seth,

I'm sure your anniversary will be a harder day. We just wanted you to know that we are continuing to pray for you. I will never forget spending time with Carol as we were getting the church set up for your wedding.

I wanted everything set up to please Carol, but Carol said, "I don't care what the church looks like. I just want to marry Seth."

What a great love you and Carol shared! Praying sweet memories can still bring happiness on your anniversary.[10]

It's never an easy task to look back through those letters and cards. In fact, each time I read them, I notice something else in each letter that I didn't catch the first few times. As I continue to grieve and grow, I have found that I see their grief in that very same struggle of loss that I was going through.

I will be the first to say that we all grieve differently and that following my example of grieving is not going to work for everyone. We all come from different lives, cultures, circumstances, faith backgrounds, and whatever other thing we would like to throw in to use as an example of how different we are, but we all grieve. I want you to know that grieving differently from how others grieve is OK, so I will continue to repeat that fact.

Keep them.

Keep the cards, messages, texts, notes, and letters. Look at them at that time, but keep them for a later point in time where you can read them for what they are really worth!

For some, words are hard to come by to offer sympathy to those grieving. Others seem to be literary geniuses and always have the right words. While some may lack the right words, we experienced some of the most heartfelt avenues of genuine care apart from cards and messages. One time it came in the form of food!

The Banana Bread

This may sound silly, but I had a batch of bananas sitting on my kitchen counter for about a week. My family goes through a lot of bananas. The boys can eat them at any time of day. The week leading up to Carol's funeral, however, everyone was bringing us so much food and snacks that the bananas sat there on the counter uneaten. I remember seeing them beginning to become overripe and thinking, *Carol would make banana bread with those*. I did nothing with them. A couple of days later, I looked at my kitchen counter, and there sat those bananas. They were just nasty. They had gotten leaky and gross, and the only thing I could do was throw them out. Just days earlier, they would have made such good banana bread.

I made a mention of those bananas in a social media post and how Carol would have already made banana bread with them. I don't remember if it was a day, two days, or more after that post when someone pulled into my driveway. It was Lil' B. Lil' B stands for Little Bailey, and she is not so little anymore. She is almost six feet tall and is a stud basketball player. She was a high school senior at the time and had already committed to go play basketball at a college. Bailey is the daughter of our good friends Toby and Jenn and had been in my youth group years before. Outside of a few times when we'd be able to visit, I hadn't seen Bailey consistently for about five years. I'm not sure why I called her Lil' B then, but sometimes things stick in my brain, and that's what it is from that point on.

Bailey saw my social media post about the bananas. Something moved within her, and she made it to my house with a gift in hand. I was going to work somewhere on the camp property as she pulled into the driveway. I met her car, not knowing it was her inside, there at the end of my driveway. She got out and walked right over to me and gave me a gift. Inside the wrapping, foil and plastic wrap, was a loaf of banana bread. She had taken the time to make me some banana bread because of the memory that I had shared. She served us in the way that she knew how, and that was so very special. Something as simple as making banana bread made my heart so full.

That was some good banana bread! More than the bread, though, I am amazed to this day how full we became in such a dire time. I am so thankful for how blessed we were to have such a supportive community surround us. I hope and pray that God reveals to you how He is working within and through those surrounding you.

Reflection: Morning Mantra Challenge

Do you have a morning mantra that you repeat each day to help you prepare for what is to come? Do you look into the mirror and tell yourself that you are good, strong, brave, courageous, kind, loving, etc.? Seriously, think about what your mornings look like. Maybe you just roll out of bed, letting the day be what it's going to be. Let's challenge your morning routine!

I encourage you to create a morning mantra or to write a letter to yourself that you can read at the start of each day. I'm not saying that we can will our day to be great, but we can prepare our minds, attitudes, and behavior to make the most of whatever our day brings. In this letter, encourage yourself, build yourself up, and acknowledge and decide that whatever unfolds during the day, you will tackle it with grace, love, and courage! Be realistic, but challenge yourself.

This may seem like a strange challenge, but the goal is two-fold. First, we align our minds and hearts with what we know is good and how God sees us. Second, we do this in hopes that we will bring goodness and joy to others. Personally, the encouragement that was brought to me through others' letters and acts of kindness after Carol's death was huge in helping me know that I was not alone. Those words and actions that I received now challenge me in how I treat others during their day.

The world and its desires pass away, but whoever does the will of God lives forever.

—1 John 2:17

CHAPTER 8
ABOUT THE "I'M FINE, WE'RE FINE"

"Hey, how are you all doing?"
"Hey, we're fine. We're making it through."
"No, really—how are you doing?"
"I'm fine. I'm making it."

I'm not sure how many times that conversation actually happened, but it was a lot. Everyone wanted to talk about how I was doing. I can't blame them for looking out for me. I think that's an awesome thing, but I wasn't always ready to talk with just anyone about the inner depths of my feelings and emotions. With some people, I didn't want to talk about it at all. I didn't even want to talk about the weather with some people at that time. It had nothing to do with them as people and everything to do with this very tragic event in my life and the lack of relationship between us.

So, I said "I'm fine" or "We're fine" when I didn't want to talk. A minister friend I once worked alongside wrote me a note validating the thought that everyone grieves differently and that it's OK to not talk at times. In the immediate aftermath of our tragedy, everyone wanted to know how we were doing. People I had never met and some whom I had just met for the first time wanted a detailed answer about how I was doing. That was my perception of the situation at the time. I don't believe that was the reality when I look back on it.

People really have no idea what to do when someone's time on earth is over. The unknown can be so incomprehensible that our minds turn to mush when thinking about it. In turn, we don't know how to react to people who have just experienced great loss either. We can find words sometimes to comfort, but, having been in the ministry for many years, I've found what is most effective is simply listening. I don't press. I don't push. I listen and only when asked do I give a response.

I found that in my time of tragedy and hurt, I preferred the way that I did things for others. Imagine that! I needed people to listen to me and just listen. I didn't need advice at that time when it came to grieving. I fully understand that people were sharing how they made it through a process because it worked for them. They were giving me a piece of themselves in their most vulnerable times, and that's special. It may not have been what I needed at that time, but it was thoughtful all the same. I so appreciate those people and their hearts. I mean, I am that person now as I'm literally telling you how I worked through the grief of losing my wife. I get that. I just didn't need it face-to-face at that time. I needed someone to come to me without an agenda. I needed someone to listen to me and not need extra details. I needed someone to respect my silence as an answer.

So, I got really good at saying, "I'm fine; we're fine." Nothing about grief is easy, despite how polished we may make it look. Hurting is not pleasant, and losing someone so close to you cuts deep. It feels as if a black hole has appeared inside your chest, sucking the life right out of you, leaving your shell of a body to go through the motions of life. You go to work, you go home, you pick up the kids from day care or school, you grocery shop—you do all these things trying to find a routine, but it all feels fake. That person was supposed to be there with you doing all those things; Carol was supposed to be there. They are not there, though, so you do them on your own; it just doesn't feel real.

So, we say, "I'm fine; we're fine" because we really don't want to talk about it. We're afraid of talking about it. Maybe you're scared of talking about it right now. When we finally say that we're not fine, it calls us into action. We are admitting the reality of the situation. We recognize that they are not here. We acknowledge that we need to heal. Maybe you don't even realize that you need to heal. Maybe you've been living in your pain for so long that you haven't grieved it yet because it has become the normal way of life now.

We have to be bigger than the "I'm fine; we're fine." We have to be OK with people seeing that we are not OK.

I have tried to pinpoint the time that I decided that I was no longer going to answer with the "I'm fine" line and just open up. I can't place it, but I've come to the point that if someone asks me about my situation and how we are doing, then I'll just be honest with them—even if they don't really want the true answer. If we are not doing well, I tell them. Now, of course, I don't give full-blown details to strangers, but I will be honest. Telling others how we feel and are truly getting along is healing. You might not believe me. You might think that it will only cause the emotions and heartache to come on strong. Those emotions may come on strong, but it is so healing to speak of what's going on behind that wall of short answers and conversation stoppers.

Why we guard our grief the ways we do is something that I still don't understand. I'm guilty of it as well. We want to be strong. Yes, I want you to be strong, too, but being strong does not equate to not grieving outwardly or not seeking help through your grief. I have always been a guarder of my feelings and emotions. I've thought, *I am a man; I need to be strong.* However, it wasn't until I felt the strength of God and the people He put around me to help me through this time that I felt the strongest. Sure, you can grieve alone, but it is not healthy and will not be a complete process. The "I'm fine; we're fine" attitude can be a toxic behavior as it is an active suppression of the very real need to release emotion after a traumatic event.

I believe that we grieve losses for our entire lives but grieve differently as more time separates us from the loss. I grieve now almost a year into my loss differently than I did two weeks after. I will grieve differently twenty years after the tragedy than I do now at a year. What each season of grief looks like past this point, I don't know. I pray, though, that as we enter into different seasons, we do so with hearts full of God's comfort as we remember our loved ones.

In my experience, joy, comfort, and peace came more easily when I recognized that I was not fine. Until I began using the tools that helped me (talking with someone, writing my thoughts and feelings out, being present in the moment), I was going nowhere in healing. I had buried my feelings. Now, at the time, I didn't know that my writing was helping me grieve. It didn't feel like talking about my feelings and thoughts was helping me. On the other hand, did I know that I was digging myself a hole by not dealing with the grief? No, I didn't. Was I aware that I was putting myself in a position of greater despair by suppressing feelings and lying to everyone that I was fine?

No, I didn't. Thankfully, I had people who would not accept that I was "fine," and they kept showing up for me.

One day, you may dig out of that hole on your own but at what cost to yourself? Lost time? Deeper wounds? Deeper hurt and loss? My journey is a flawed one, but recognizing that I was not fine allowed the work to begin in me that was already working around me. Only then could I begin working through the layers of acceptance, self-realization, denial, depression, fear, confusion, and healing. When we do that, suddenly joy, comfort, and peace seem to be readily available. If we refuse to walk through our loss and hurt, our grief will control us to the day that we die. I pray you walk with the Lord by your side leading you through that valley of the shadow of death; I pray it is also with the body of Christ alongside you.

Reflection: No Shortcuts

Have you ever thought, *I wish all this grief would just go away?* I think most of us have.

I remember playing video games as a kid. Who am I kidding? I still play video games! One of my favorite games was Super Mario Bros. on the Nintendo (NES). We're talking about the 1990s. When playing this game, there are certain shortcuts that you can take to skip multiple worlds in the game. It's an easy way to not only finish the game more quickly but also skip a world or two that you might not like. What I found, though, is that when I played the game in its entirety and didn't take the shortcuts, it obviously took longer, but I was better at playing the game.

We might want to bury our grief and act as if it's not there, but when we walk through it, we grow and become something new. It might be a difficult level of life, but it is going to help you through all the levels that are still to come.

Trust in the Lord with all your heart
    and lean not on your own understanding;
in all your ways submit to him,
    and he will make your paths straight.

                          —Proverbs 3:5–6

CHAPTER 9
ABOUT THE REST OF THE WORLD

Our worlds crashed while the rest of the world kept on as usual. Their lives didn't change dramatically that day as ours did. Some of them for sure have thought often about Carol. Some of them may have memories come flooding back when something they see or have heard reminds them of Carol, but their lives for the most part did not change like the lives of those who loved her as a wife, mother, daughter, sister, or close friend have. It is OK that it didn't change their daily lives.

The world keeps moving even when you and I are not roaming this earth. Maybe that's a hard thought to comprehend but not when we remove the "self" from everything. We often think of the world with us at the center of it. They say the same thing about babies, toddlers, and younger elementary children who haven't grown that portion of their brains or self-awareness yet. Their worlds revolve around themselves, and nothing exists outside of them. I believe anyone who has had children or works with children of those ages knows that not much else matters to the child besides what they want and when they want it.

We also live in a world where recognition and fame are often the things sought after most. One reality of life is the certainty that it will end one day. That is tough to swallow.

The truth of the matter is, though, as I said before, the rest of the world keeps moving even when someone close to you passes. Friends and family go back home to their own lives. Your career would like to have you back. The kids still need to be schooled. Birthdays keep coming around. Holidays don't take a break either. Bills still fill the mailbox. The world just keeps going even when our personal lives have been shattered and broken. Even when the pieces are still lying on the floor yet to be swept up, the sun comes up and the sun goes down.

How do you process that? How did I process that? It's as if the world came to my side when my wife passed and during the following weeks, but when it was time for people to go back to their own lives is when the loss felt the most real. In that moment, I was afraid of people forgetting about Carol. I want so desperately for her legacy to live on. I know it will, but in those first few weeks when the people left and I knew that the world was continuing to move forward and that we would keep making trips around the sun, I feared that people would forget Carol. That was a hard thought and feeling for me to work through. Maybe you've feared that the world will forget your loved one as well. How will you let their legacy live on through you?

I've lived my grief out loud. It wasn't intentional to be so public about my grief and how we were processing it all and living life through it. Rather, it came about so organically. Initially, I just wanted the memory of Carol to stay alive, so I was posting pictures and memories. I had just lost my best friend, and I wanted everyone to know what the world had lost. It wasn't until I started posting on social media about my grief and different writings about missing Carol and how the boys and I were coping with it all that I realized that by posting those things I was grieving through them. I equate it to spending time in therapy. I do believe that because I've been intentional about not hiding the grieving process that it has helped me work through hard emotions and feelings. Writing has helped tremendously.

One outcome of this type of journaling is that it has made me acknowledge that the world is going to move on from Carol's death. People are used to others coming and going in their lives, and unless you were close to that person, you won't feel the loss that greatly. A few will feel the impact, but many won't. It is the reality of a busy world. That does not make them bad people. In fact, it doesn't make you a bad person either for acknowledging that you, too, will move forward and take further steps of healing. Unless our lives move forward, we cannot heal.

Let me give you two examples of how the world keeps moving. The first is not about the death of a loved one but more about the end to a season of life, and the second is more of what could be still to come in life.

The Church

We had moved back to central Missouri nine months before Carol's passing. We had departed from a wonderful church in west central Illinois where we had seen so much growth. Our family had grown by two more humans. Our marriage had grown so much closer. Serving at our church in Illinois was one of the best seasons of ministry that we had been a part of. Carol grew so much spiritually there. Her knowledge of the Bible, her longing to follow Christ even more closely, and her desire to further her role in God's kingdom grew exponentially.

Having had two boys fifteen months apart, growing our family to five humans, and my position continuing to need me gone for weeks at a time in the summer and for different trips, we came to the prayerful conclusion that God was ending my time in that ministry. Our season of leading in the church was coming to a close, and we felt that we were transitioning into a new season of being a part of the church rather than leading it. That may sound strange, but taking part in something is different from leading something; it's a totally different focus.

After acknowledging our season of life and spending time in prayer, we took on an awesome position just thirty minutes from where I grew up in Missouri. We promptly entered into a season of being a part of a church, of being fed and led, rather than leading it.

Do you know what happened at the church in Illinois that we had left? After I had spent countless hours preparing, leading, teaching, praying, sweating, traveling, and spending multiple years assisting in its growth and spiritual health, the church hired someone else. And that is exactly what they were supposed to do. You know, I've never left a job and had that place say, "We're retiring that position because Seth is no longer here." It's never happened. The church had to keep moving. For the healthy future of that church, they needed to be in action. For the success of that church, they needed to acknowledge where they were at and move forward.

For the health of the boys and me, we must also be in action just as our last church was after we left. We must acknowledge that "living" in sadness of the memories of what the past had will not allow us to appreciate in the future the memories of what we had. My two youngest children may not remember any moments that they had with their mother, and that breaks my heart. What would break my heart even more, though, is if they never saw me happy and saw me only living in sadness with the memories that I had. I choose to live now and let them see me happy. Any memories that they have of their mommy will be of me telling them those memories, and if I speak of her only in sadness, sadness is what they will know and always associate with their mother. I don't want her memory reduced to sadness when she was so much bigger and more special than the end of her life. They need to see me living life. We choose to live in the present because only then can the memories of what we had be looked at with joy rather than complete sadness.

The rest of the world will move on, and those of us grieving will be tempted to not move forward. Don't fall into that trap. We can move forward honoring our loved one's memory and the legacy that they left. There is more to come in our stories if we still have breath in our bodies.

The Blessing

There's an account of a guy named Job in the Bible. I once did a character study on Job for a college course assignment. The story of Job is fascinating and terrifying at the same time. Job had everything. He had family, land, livestock, workers, money, friends, respect—he had it all. Then, one day and in the days following, he lost everything he had. His family died. His livestock was destroyed. His land was ravaged. He was sick. He lost everything that was good to him and for him (Job 1). The world looked at Job in his despair and maybe felt for him for a little while. His friends, for a while at least, came to Job and sat with him. It appears that they weren't sure how to handle Job's losses either. They sat in silence as Job mourned and grieved for seven days, but then they opened their mouths and offered bad advice. Did they offer that bad advice thinking it was good advice? In my experience, people offer any advice (bad or good) when they don't know what to say and many times lack the wisdom to remain silent. Their understanding, tactfulness, and methods were clearly incorrect when they told Job that his suffering was a result of all that he had done wrong. It is obvious that they cared about Job and his well-being initially, but they also wanted to explain away Job's suffering in order for it to end and to move on. They wanted the suffering to stop for him; they simply weren't equipped to handle his grief or their own. After being rebuked by God because of their lack of wisdom and understanding of God, they left Job (Job 42:7–9).

I felt a lot like Job at the time of my loss. Tragedy happened. People came. They grieved with me and offered some advice. They left, and I still had grief to deal with.

Carol passed on a Friday. A week before she passed, a severe storm came and ravaged the camp property that we managed. Our property was just wrecked. The week after Carol's passing, Covid-19 spread through a church that came to the camp for a week and then at the camp as well. I don't know how many times we were exposed to Covid-19 at Carol's funeral, but we were exposed many times. At her funeral, there were tornadoes in the area, much like the tornadoes that swept Job's family and workers away. I was mentally exhausted and spiritually empty with sickness, destruction, and loss all around me. I felt as if I knew what Job had felt on some minor level. My world stood still as the rest of the world looked on and soon would move on. I had better friends than Job did though. I had plenty of people who wanted to offer their advice, but I found comfort in those who sat with me and let me mourn. I pray that you have people who will sit in silence and mourn with you and not try to fix your problems. Grief is not something to be fixed but something that we work through.

I remember telling my friend Tommy, who is a minister I have been friends with for many years, that I felt a lot like Job in his time of great loss and grief. I first met Tommy at the camp I managed. Tommy dropped everything that he was doing and showed up to just be there for me. He was there to grieve, mourn, and work through the funeral process with me. I appreciated that very much. I wish everyone could have a Tommy to be there for them and to walk through the process with them. After I told Tommy how I felt like Job, I was taken back by what he said in response to my asking, "What's next?"

I told him, "Now, I don't equate myself to having the righteousness that Job had, but I just feel like Job, and I keep wondering to myself, 'What is going to happen to me next?'" Tommy probably doesn't even remember that he said this, but I've held on to what he said to this day. He said it so quickly and with so much conviction:

"The blessing."

He said, "The blessing." Maybe the blessing was next.

I'm not sure what I said in response, but I know what I was thinking internally, *I really am like Job. I'm not like Job because of my troubles but because of a speech that Job gives to God.* You see, Job was very intent on not cursing God and on remaining faithful throughout his whole ordeal, but he gave this speech to God about the situation and all that had happened to him and how it all happened under God's watch (Job 29–31). God responded to Job by putting him in his place (Job 38:1–40:2; 40:6–41:34). Following God's speech, Job's final response to God comes in Job 42:1–6.

> Then Job replied to the Lord:
>> "I know that you can do all things;
>>> no purpose of yours can be thwarted.
>> You asked, 'Who is this that obscures my plans without
>>> knowledge?'
>> Surely I spoke of things I did not understand,
>>> things too wonderful for me to know.
>>
>> You said, 'Listen now, and I will speak;
>>> I will question you,

and you shall answer me.'
My ears had heard of you
    but now my eyes have seen you.
Therefore I despise myself
    and repent in dust and ashes."

"Therefore I despise myself and repent in dust and ashes."
In that moment, Job knew that God was in control, and he resolved himself to that truth; he accepted God's control even when his world was crushed. In that same chapter we find that God blessed Job even greater than He had before. The blessing came after the trial. It required Job to see and acknowledge that even though his world had been shattered, God was still working and was still in control of His creation. It was in the moment that he acknowledged who sits on the throne that Job began to live and move forward. The world may have moved on before Job, but Job was now living with purpose and greater faith.

In fact, it is after this acknowledgment of God *and* after Job begins being a blessing to others by praying for them that we read of Job's own blessings.

I believe I have been greatly blessed. There is nothing in the future that can take away or minimize the joy of having had Carol as my wife, my boys' mother, and my best friend. I believe having had her in my life will only magnify what God has set for our future.

Just like it was for Job, though, it was and is essential that we acknowledge that God is still in control, that God is still good, and that God is still working in our lives. It is when we do this that we can accept that the rest of the world keeps moving, that it's OK that the world keeps moving, and that it's OK for us to move forward as well.

When Tommy responded that day in the parking lot of a restaurant that we had just eaten at with those two words—*the blessing*—it was a blessing. Those two words comforted me not because I now expected a blessing but because it was a solid reminder to me that God was still in control. Whether I am blessed further or not, I hope to bless others each day and be some sort of help for others who have a story similar to my own. Maybe my blessing comes in the form of blessing others and walking alongside them in their grief.

Reflection: Moving Forward

Job better understood who God was after the tragic events in his life. I imagine that he would have wanted to learn that lesson in a different way, but that is not how it played out. I believe I am not the only one who can relate to how Job felt in the aftermath of his loss, how he felt that he had done everything right yet was still allowed to suffer. Based on my own journey and my study of Job's story, I've concluded that moving forward.

- is not denying the pain and sadness we've experienced; it is choosing to live with joy.

- is not rushing through the grief process; it is finding hope even amid the grieving.

- is not having a full understanding of why God allows things to happen; it is accepting and believing in God's sovereignty.

- is not dismissing the value of what or who we have lost; it is receiving new blessings.

- is not forgetting our loved one; it is choosing to honor our loved one's legacy.

Even though the fig trees have no blossoms,
  and there are no grapes on the vines;
even though the olive crop fails,
  and the fields lie empty and barren;
even though the flocks die in the fields,
  and the cattle barns are empty,
yet I will rejoice in the Lord!
  I will be joyful in the God of my salvation!
The Sovereign Lord is my strength!
  He makes me as surefooted as a deer,
  able to tread upon the heights.

—Habakkuk 3:17–19 NLT

CHAPTER 10
ABOUT WHAT'S NEXT

It was while I was standing in the visitation line that I first heard someone question my future. It's not that I hadn't asked God, "What am I supposed to do now?" but to have others ask what was next was such a weird experience. The timing of that question, as mentioned before, was quite strange, but now that it's been more than a year since I was standing in that visitation line, the question looms differently. Initially, the question was more along the lines of "How will we make it through the event?" Comprehending a future without Carol was hard to think about, but as time separated us from the tragedy, it became easier to have hope of a bright future or even new companionship. Her continued absence from my daily life was the constant reminder that allowed me to begin thinking differently about my future. While that line of thinking comes with guilt, even though it shouldn't, each day I am more convinced that she would not want me to live life without companionship or happiness. What comes next is a scary thought because it is not just my future I have to think about; I also have the boys to consider. I'm guessing that it's scary for you as well to figure out what's next after losing a loved one. While I won't ask you that question at your loved one's funeral, I will challenge you to think about what is next. I want to encourage you to just take a glimpse at what can be in your future and to consider how you can keep on healing while moving forward.

The Possibilities

Have you ever been given the freedom to create on a blank canvas? Maybe that blank canvas was a new job opportunity, a house renovation, a raw piece of land, or even a literal blank canvas. The possibilities of what can be are endless. Let's take the idea of a literal blank canvas. It's clean, crisp, and new. A little bit of paint and the stroke of a brush can transform that blank canvas into something else completely. A splatter of paint instead of the brushstroke can give that blank canvas an even different form of beauty. Foam brushes, charcoal pencils, and even crayons can transform that canvas into something great. What doesn't transform that blank piece into something greater is doing nothing with it. If it's left on the easel, it collects dust, becomes faded, and is lost to new projects. The hope of something new, bright, and fulfilling is lost on us when we refuse to think about what may come next in our lives.

That's how I'm approaching this season of my grief journey. When I say "clean" and "new," I'm talking about the opportunity itself. I, on the other hand, as the painter and creator, am messy and torn. I am a widower, a father of three young boys who's broken by the loss of my wife, but despite that messiness and weariness, a clean and crisp canvas full of opportunities is before me. My experiences with grief, sadness, joy, love, and life along the way can and will help create something that is fully me and something fully new. I—we—have to move forward.

There is no timeline to follow. While we talk about new relationships, new experiences, and all things "new" to us, there is no set schedule. There are steps to grieving, but we don't need to rush. We should progress with every intention of moving forward when we can as appropriate. Many of us move through the stages of grief without knowing it. Some handle grief better than others. Some refuse to grieve (denial is a part of grieving). Others try to downplay their grief. It stands true whether we accept it or not that we all grieve; we just grieve differently. My hope is that although you grieve, there is intentionality with it. When talking about the possibilities of what may be next, we aren't talking about an endgame to your grieving but a life being lived while continuing to heal and grieve.

New Relationships

Moving forward from something that was such a great part of you for so long is a difficult task (and reality) to take on. That's why the question of what to do next is so hard after the loss. I mentioned that moving forward comes with guilt for me, and I have a suspicion that it does for many others as well. On what would have been my anniversary, I posted the following on social media:

August 9, 2022

Fourteen years ago on August 9th, 2008, Carol Crowe married Seth Tyler.

What used to be celebration on these special dates now leads to thinking and remembering what used to be. It's also now just shy of fourteen months since Carol passed. I think with time, though, the other days without special designation have become more hopeful about what can be and generally less sad. We've tried to do what I believe Carol would want us to do—that is, to live life to the full.

Today is one of those specially designated days—our anniversary date. I think today about what our marriage meant and celebrate the many years that we had to build our marriage together. I think about those vows that we took fourteen years ago.

" . . . to have and to hold from this day forward, for better or for worse, for richer, for poorer, in sickness and in health, to love and to cherish from this day forward until death do us part."

It's so strange that those vows were kept in full. Not in the sense that it's crazy that we kept our vows to each other but the part at the end. The part where it says "until death do us part"—that's the strange part. That completion of the vows is what stings the most.

The commitments, or vows, expressed before that phrase with the declaration of death may be difficult to live up to, but they are things we say with the hope of making it through them. We want and hope to make it through the hard, sick, and poor times together. The finality of the last phrase "until death do us part" is easy to say, but until you experience and realize that there is no more "from this day forward" in your relationship after death—it's a hard truth to live in, knowing that the completion of those vows has taken place. You might say that it's a no-brainer that there is no more "from this day forward" after death, but it's a realization that I wouldn't wish upon anyone.

Death ends the commitment that you set out to keep. The commitment to be there for each other, to support one another, and live out life alongside the other has been fulfilled by way of the one's death. When we use that last phrase in our vows, we think of growing old together and holding each other's hands as we peacefully pass in our sleep side by side. It's strange that the realities of life hit us hard when death has taken place.

My intention in talking about this is not to make you afraid of what could be but the opposite. My intention is for you to feel the need to embrace all that you have in your companion while you live out your vows that you expressed to each other—hopefully for many, many years to come.

So much about marriage is the companionship it involves. It's not just about the physical intimacy, the having and holding, that comes with companionship but the living life through those times that are better and the times that are worse. I'm so thankful that we didn't waste our time together. Never were we rich with monetary wealth (definitely poor), but we were rich with experience, family, and love. We were no stranger to sickness in our family, but we also knew good health. It is without a doubt that we loved and cherished each other. That companionship is grown and elevated when you experience both sides of the beginning set of vows. Those experiences solidify a committed marriage. Embrace each other as you face both sides of those vows and know that you will be stronger and your marriage strengthened even in the harder times . . . especially in the harder times.

There is a phrase, in my opinion, in those vows that isn't true; I know this now.

Maybe the placement of a few words or even an addition of a word or two needs to be changed or made to make it a truer statement. Whoever wrote those vows had never experienced the loss of a spouse but only the brightness of what the future would hold with their soon-to-be spouse. I would change them, the vows, to be something more like the following.

". . . to have and to hold from this day forward, for better or for worse, for richer, for poorer, in sickness and in health, from this day forward until death do us part. I will love and cherish you for the rest of my days."

It's just a minor change in words, a simple rearrangement and small addition, but it's more realistic—"I will love and cherish you for the rest of my days" as a statement all on its own after the declaration of death do us part.

Granted, where there is death you can no longer enjoy "to have and hold." There is no better or worse or rich or poor. There is no more in sickness or in health. Yet, there still is love for your missing partner. You still love and cherish them, and I don't believe that goes away when death shows up; I think you always do love them.

You still love them and will for the rest of your days. You cherish their memory. That doesn't take away from any love that you may give to your friends or family or to another if God has that in your future. There will just always be a part of you that loves the one you lost.

On this day, our anniversary date, I'm so thankful for the companionship that we had. I miss it. I've said it a thousand times, but I'll say it again: I miss my best friend. Even though I don't get to have and hold her anymore, I will always love her. I will cherish the memories that we made—even the "for poorer" and "in sickness" and "for worse."

This day will always be our anniversary date and have meaning in my life.

For the rest of my days, my heart will have a love for Carol that few are able to receive from me in my lifetime.[11]

While it is true that her death ended that commitment, moving forward in a new relationship almost feels as if I would be committing some great sin against Carol and our relationship. That line of thinking is simply false. I accept that I am wrong in my feelings, and I hope that you do as well. God created us to have community, companionship, and a life of joy.

There are many things to consider in moving forward with new relationships (whether with a significant other or people in general). I have to take into account the boys. Anyone in this position with children should keep their feelings, grief, and future in consideration as well. They, the kids, are not the decision-makers but will be impacted by the decisions that are made going forward, just as they were when their other parent was living. When going into new relationships, don't forgo your existing relationships (especially with your children) for something new. Their input matters. They, the kids, might not be ready for you to be in a new relationship, and while that decision is not up to them, they may need you to listen to their feelings. This would be a perfect opportunity to talk with your kids about how you feel and specifically of your need for friends and companionship as well.

I've been asked many times, "Will you marry again?" In fact, I was asked that question in person soon after my loss. I was asked that question in a coffee shop point-blank. In defense of the one who asked the question, it came almost a year after Carol passed, and the person was trying to figure out if I was ready for a relationship because she had a friend in mind to introduce me to. I've been asked on social media. In fact, my own son asked it while we were in the family car heading to the cemetery after the funeral. He meant nothing by it, and I quickly told him to "Shhhhh!" as Carol's family was in the car with us. I think he was worried about it and asked. At first, I thought it was forbidden for me to talk about any future relationships. I felt that everyone else was having that discussion for me, but I wasn't allowed to be a part of it. Here's the thing about this question, it's real and raw and approaches the "What's next?" I don't have an answer for it yet, but I do know now that it is not a forbidden topic and one that does not warrant guilt or fear. Don't be afraid to consider the future. Considering the future reveals healing in the grieving process.

New Experiences

I am thankful that I live in the area that I originally grew up in. I'm also thankful that I live near the town in which we laid Carol to rest. As mentioned in another chapter, I can visit Carol's grave at any time that I choose to do so. One day I might not live in this town because of new opportunities. How do I reconcile that with being able to visit her? The truth of that line of thinking is that while I do visit often, I think of her just as often whether I'm going to the cemetery or not. There may come a time that an opportunity presents itself to better myself and my boys, and I must accept the realization that taking on new experiences does not lessen the bond, relationship, life, love, experiences, and joy that we had together. The same goes for you and your loved one. I am convinced in my case that the three questions that Carol would ask when it comes to big decisions like taking on new experiences or opportunities are:

1. Have you prayed about it?
2. Have you tested it against Scripture?
3. Do you have peace about it?

Number two may seem strange to use, but whenever we came up against something that had us unsure of which direction to go, we would see what Scripture had to say about it. It might not have spoken about our problem at hand directly, but seeking God out in that decision-making process allowed us to be sure that we were inside His will. So, I do the same now. When taking on new opportunities and experiences, I pray about it. I seek out God's Word on the matter (love after love lost; boys in public school, private school, or homeschool; stay where we are or start something new; and the list goes on). I also try to be self-aware, noticing whether I have peace about it or not.

All Things New . . . or Renewed

I used to run for fun. I wasn't running from a bear, to beat another person, or to lose weight. Of course, I would record my running times for reference, I enjoyed beating other people if I was in a local race, and I did lose weight because of it. However, my primary motivation was that I enjoyed running. Once we had kids, I didn't get to run as much. We did other things, but that hobby or form of "fun" running hadn't been as regular in my life. I recently started running for enjoyment again. Now, the actual act of running hasn't been enjoyable each time simply because I'm not in shape like I was, but the experience of renewing something that used to be a part of me is exciting. There is something joyful about renewing an old hobby.

Early on in our marriage, I tried new hobbies, including starting several collections. I've collected many things, ranging from old cameras to sports cards to jewelry. While most of those have faded, I did start a new collection as a hobby. Now I collect Kansas City Royals bobbleheads. I am a Kansas City Royals fan, and my basement, which is painted blue, gray, and white, is a reflection of that. Our in-home library is on one wall of the basement, and a center showpiece of that library is a picture of Kauffman Stadium framed in old barn wood. On the top shelf of our library from one wall to the other are my Kansas City Royals bobbleheads of different players. My favorite bobblehead is of George Brett's famous charge from the dugout when they ejected him for having tar "too high" on his bat, which led to the Royals temporarily losing the game. My next favorite is of Alex Gordon with his finger pointing high in the sky as he had just hit the game-tying ninth-inning solo home run of the first game of the 2015 World Series. Collecting bobbleheads has become a new hobby for me and one that has multiple ways of fulfillment. I get to search out the prize, make a deal, and display my collection. This has been a way that has helped in making something that was both of ours (our basement) into something that is new for me and shows forward progress, even if it is just decorating a place to call my own. Are there spaces or activities that you can make your own that would aid in your healing process?

I shared two things, running and my bobblehead collection, that are fairly simple but have aided in me becoming a new form of me in the now and present. What is it for you? What new or renewed thing is now helping you become a new form of you going forward? You are not forgetting the past by moving forward but building on what was to help form what is or what can be.

Renewed Focus

A part of what is going to fuel and propel us into what is next is having a renewed and intentional focus on each part of our health—our physical, mental, and spiritual health.

Physical Health

I call it the "widower's weight." Personally, I gained weight after Carol passed. I've read of people not eating and call it "widow's weight loss." Whether we have gained or lost weight, it is often a result of us not taking care of ourselves in our time of grief. There is a lot to say about physical health, but the one thing that I want us to recognize is that our physical health, mental health, and spiritual health all affect one another. To be successful in keeping up our physical health while experiencing deep grief will take intentionality, but doing so will aid us in healthy grieving.

Off and on during our marriage, I gained weight and then lost weight. As I said previously, I took up running early on in our marriage, and it kept me in fairly good shape. I love to run. Life would happen, though, and the weight would creep back on. Then I'd realize it and lose the weight again. I took up Cross-Fit and really enjoyed doing that form of exercise and weight lifting. I was dedicated to it and was feeling really healthy. And then Carol's life ended.

I didn't work out from that day on, except for a handful of times, for at least six months. Widower's weight followed. My life with three boys just sped up in that time, and my physical health paid the price. Other people would bring over stuff to eat. Fast food was easier than cooking. A cake here and a cake there seemed to match better with my emotions and grieving than the healthy stuff that I used to eat. I even hired a nutritionist at one point because I needed the help to get back on track. She was great, and I may use her services in the future, but it just didn't jive with the speed that my life was going in after suddenly becoming a single parent. I was struggling in a big way, and in no time, I had gained at least twenty pounds.

Another thing that didn't help us is that the boys just kept getting sick from the new germs at day care. It wasn't the day care's fault. The boys were just being introduced to new germs, and it was a constant back and forth to day care and then the doctor. It wasn't helping them that we would stop by a drive-through for food, but it was so much easier. Camp was also in session, and we would eat the camp food. Now, there is nothing wrong with camp food for a week, but a summer's worth gets old, and it isn't always the healthiest.

My goal since I acknowledged that widower's weight gain has been to make everything simple. Using the acronym KISS (from the old saying, "Keep it simple, stupid") and making routines for us has been pivotal in our attempt to make healthy changes. I use the slow cooker and air fryer and steam veggies in the microwave. We try to follow the same routines each day to help the boys and keep the consistency of what they are doing. It also helps me exponentially; it allows me to know what is coming up and how much time I have for something, so I can schedule events easily. I don't have to try to remember everything that I need to do because I'm prepared for what I need to do. I've scheduled. I've planned. I'm disciplined. I'm prepared. This is some of what it takes to be in good health.

Below is a list to recap what I'm doing to get in better physical health. Remember that good physical health along with sound mental health and spiritual health can aid us in healthy grieving.

- **Be intentional.** I've landed on this process of being intentional about what I'm doing. It requires us to see what we are eating. It requires us to get out of bed, put our feet on the floor, lace up our shoes, and actively move with purpose. It requires us to be self-aware of what we are doing in hopes of having not only better physical health but also better mental and spiritual health. Being intentional with what we are doing allows us to know where we are, how far we've come, and how far we have yet to go. Accidental success is not the normal route to being successful. Be purposeful with everything that you do. It will help you have some control over what you are doing during your time of grieving.

- **Keep it simple.** I've simplified our routines, meals, and schedules. Keeping it simple is going to help in that immediate time of grief and allow you to ease into the normal speed of life. For example, make mealtimes easy. We purchased kitchen tools that would make preparing food easier for us. We use quick-and-easy recipes.

- **Implement routines.** Routines help everyone involved. A routine allows you to grieve and still keep your commitments. It gives you a time, thing, or event to focus your energy and emotion on.

- **Choose healthy foods.** We eliminated—almost—our fast-food drive-through visits.

Slowly but surely, I have been able to lose this "widower's weight." Making one small, good decision after the next will pay off. Consistency, discipline, and dedication will produce positive results. You can have success too. This list can transfer over to other areas of your life as well.

Mental Health

Mental health is an emerging topic in today's world simply because it was thought of in a negative light for so long. Now that we have brought mental health issues to the forefront of public discussion, it has become an acceptable topic. Depression, anger, self-harm, and suicidal thoughts are talked about daily, but just a few years ago people were afraid to admit that they were dealing with such things. Mental health awareness is so prevalent now that there is rarely a day that we do not see or hear a commercial on the radio, television, or social media addressing it. Grieving the loss of a loved one affects your mental health. There's no way around it. When someone close to you passes, it affects every part of you. Something you see on TV, the restaurant where you had your first date, or the ball field where you watched your child play sports may remind you of your loss. There are triggers all around us that can put our minds in a state of sadness and despair. Simply put, we have to address what to do in those situations.

This is the only place in this book that I give you how-to type of advice on grieving after experiencing loss. Again, I am not a mental health professional, and this is based solely on my personal experience through grief.

- **Have at least one meeting with someone trained in grief counseling.** Maybe you are not part of a church that has a minister who has walked many people through grief. Maybe you aren't part of a church at all. Either way, a minister within your community can get you in touch with a grief counselor or someone trained in walking people through grief. It is scary to allow yourself to be vulnerable with someone. It's even more frightening when you may not know that person in the least bit. For myself, speaking to someone about my feelings, fears, and pain was something that I had never truly done. Outside of communicating those things to my wife, I didn't feel the need to do so before. The freedom that comes with opening yourself up for help far outweighs the fear of being judged in those conversations. I am not a failure for struggling through the loss of my wife and seeking help. In fact, had I failed to seek help, I believe my struggles would have been greater.

- **Find a healthy outlet for your thoughts and feelings.** I have found that nothing has helped me cope with confusion, uneasiness, restlessness, and pain more than using my social media posts as an outlet to get my thoughts and feelings out of my head.

- **Keep a journal.** It seems that I just keep suggesting this, doesn't it? This goes along with finding a healthy outlet. You do not have to start your journal with "Dear diary," but having a place to collect your inner thoughts provides a sense of control in an uncontrollable situation.

- **Surround yourself with people who have your best interests at heart.** It's strange to say, but there are people who live off drama and are weirdly energized by your pain. Their need to know everything can feel like a great release for you but could prove detrimental when there is no more to tell them. It is important to have a sound mind near you during grief. Whether that sound mind comes from a counselor, minister, friend, or mentor, they need to have your best interest at heart. That means that they are there for you—not for your pain and suffering but to walk alongside you. I would suggest the first place to look is your church family.

- **Take time for yourself.** Take a "you day" every now and then. Find something that offers peace and sit in it for a day.

Spiritual Health

I would be lying if I said that losing Carol didn't strengthen my faith in a loving God. I know that this statement sounds crazy, but it is true. I might have cried out to God "Why?" and maybe even blamed Him as I searched for answers in moments of despair. But, ultimately, I don't blame God for taking Carol. We live in a world full of sickness, destruction, sadness, and loss. It's hard to expect anything more from a fading and temporary world. I'm fallible and selfish—I wish it didn't happen, but it did. As hard as it has been to accept, God has been anything but distant. By all evidence, God has been only love to my family. My family and I would not be where we are today if it weren't for the constant care and provision of God through His body, the church. What I do now and in this time of waiting for God to reveal what He is doing in our lives is most important.

Spiritual health is just as important as the other two facets of health. This one may be a harder one to approach though. What constitutes spiritual health? Who is to say that one person is spiritually healthier than another? Maybe there is no way to dive into one's faith and adequately determine if they are healthy or not. Biblically, a spiritually healthy person produces fruit. That makes sense. When a tree or plant is healthy, it will produce fruit. When a person is spiritually healthy, that testimony will bear fruit in their lives. Keeping with the same line of thought, there are seasons that a tree or plant may not produce as much as the year before or the year to come. This is called alternate bearing. In the horticulture world, alternate bearing is typical of fruit trees. One season's fruit will be plentiful, while the next year will have less harvest. Maybe when we are grieving, we are in an alternate-bearing season. There may be less fruit, but when I said that it matters what we do in this period of grieving and in the time of waiting for God to reveal His plan for us, it wasn't just to fill a page with words. The crazy thing about this alternate bearing is that the next year's bountiful harvest begins in that off year. What we do now matters. Use this time as a break, catch your breath, and begin to move forward, aligning yourself with God's will. It's not easy, but surrendering yourself daily to His will allows growth to take place. This next season may be plentiful and productive.

I visited a church, and they were going through a series called "Encounters." These encounters were between Jesus and someone in the Bible. Each week before the sermon, they put a testimony video of a member within that church and showed it to all in attendance. The week I was visiting, the church showed a video of a teenager who had dealt with some mental health issues, exhaustion, and desperation. One night, she came to a point where she cried out to God to prove that He was there and real. There was no audible response. There was no angel coming down from heaven; no spectacular, tangible show of God's power came down to prove it. God did answer though. It was through peace. She said that a consuming peace overwhelmed her after she cried out to God. Her next line in the testimony video was my favorite. She said, "I basically just fell asleep after that." I don't think she knew how important that sentence was as she went on with her testimony. The young woman cried out to God and she received God's peace in an overwhelming presence. Rest followed God's peace.

For our spiritual health we need to know that (1) God is working in, through, and all around us, and we need to seek Him out; (2) some seasons won't look as bright and plentiful as others, but they do propel us forward into another plentiful season; and (3) rest is needed, and God provides it.

(Re)Prioritize Our Values

What is most important to you? What do you want to be remembered for? Do you know who you are? What are things that you like? What is on your bucket list? What is something that you've always wanted to do and found yourself never going after? Ask yourself questions like these to help figure out who you are and what you want. Maybe it'll be the first time you prioritize values, or maybe you'll re-prioritize values as an individual after loss.

These are just some of the questions that I've asked myself as I am the sole person choosing what I do now. For fourteen years, it was not just me making decisions but us. It is inevitable that we lose some of who we are as individuals to become who "we" are as a couple over that period of time. That is not a bad thing. As we compromise our earthly desires, we benefit and grow into something greater than we once were as individuals. Our answers to these questions will differ as we have different circumstances. I will make decisions with my boys as my first priority. It probably stands to reason that I can't just up and go backpacking through Europe no matter how fun that might sound. I can, however, load up the truck with my boys and go hiking at a state park or travel a few states over and get up in the mountains. I also find that it is a priority that the boys and I are in church regularly and not just going to church but being the church. Volunteering is something that I view as important. It goes on the list of priorities. Self-care is important to me. It goes on the list of priorities. Being active is important to me. It goes on the list of priorities. Spending time with family is important to me. It goes on the list of priorities. Talking to other adults my age is important to me. It goes on the list of priorities.

Do you see a theme here? What we find to be important in our lives needs to be made a priority to us. Knowing who you are and what you want takes away the guesswork in what's next for you as you continue to grieve and heal. It sets a plan to come back to. It may change over time as you grow and mature in your grief and, hopefully, move forward in a healthy fashion.

Choose to Live

What can I do that best honors the life of my loved one? The answer: choose to live.

We honor our loved ones by allowing ourselves to be free to live our lives to the full. How do I plan on honoring the life of my loved one? I land on living life to the full.

I lead a community group at our church. A friend of mine in the group used a very simple phrase when talking about a rough patch in his life. I have thought often about four words that he spoke as he gave a bit of his testimony. In fact, I have daily recited those four words since that group session and am convinced that there is a need to share it with you as well. My friend is an A-10 pilot in the air force and, by all accounts, is a stud fighter jet pilot. When talking to him in person, his demeanor does not match the fighter pilot persona that Hollywood offers us. He is soft-spoken and humble, and he uses his words carefully as not to misspeak. That night at our community group he said during a rough time in his life he was talking with a grandparent of his and telling them all about his circumstances, not knowing what he should do in the situation. "Witness on the way"—that was the advice that was given to him. Witness for Christ on the way to the next destination, through the issues, as we try to find our way back to something that resembles normalcy. These are the four words that have gripped my thoughts since that night when I've thought about what's next for us. This is the advice that I give you. You witness on the way. I witness on the way. We witness on the way. When the destination is unknown, when we feel overwhelmed by all that is going on, when we aren't sure if this grief will ever lessen, we witness on the way. Even when, especially when, we think things are coming together and we have a good feel for life and the direction it's heading, we witness on the way. We make it known that God is still in control, that He is still on His throne, and that He is still good.

It's important for us to have goals to strive to obtain. It's important for us to continue to live life! My goal has been the same since beginning this project, but I now finally have the right words to describe what it is that I have been trying to do since the morning after Carol's death. I have been trying to witness on the way. Even when I feel that God has not given a destination and I am in a period of waiting, I will witness in the wait. I will witness of His faithfulness. I will witness of His great love, grace, peace, and comfort. I will witness of His victory over death and the hope of a future. However it may be, on the way or in the wait, the goal is to glorify God in all that I do. There will be seasons that are consumed with rest, but in those seasons, I will witness of what He has done and what He has promised to do. That is how I choose to live, and I hope that you do the same!

Reflection: Good Things Are Still Possible

It's scary to think about what comes next, isn't it? We've experienced a loss so deep that imagining something new isn't possible for us, is it? As much as I can relate to that last sentence, new things *are* possible. It is possible to contemplate what's next. It is possible to reestablish yourself. You do not have to live in sadness. You may grieve for the rest of your life, but grief doesn't have to be overwhelmingly sad and stagnant.

I have found that if I live in sadness, then I am not living. I don't want to negate the times of sadness, but I challenge you to be willing to acknowledge that there will be a time when you can put one foot in front of the other and make headway in your healing. There can still be good to come in your life!

I challenge you to pause for a moment and just breathe. Now, list just one thing that is good in your life. Pause for another moment and breathe. Now, list another good thing in your life. Repeat three more times.

I have told you these things, so that in me you may have peace. In this world you will have trouble. But take heart! I have overcome the world.

—John 16:33

CHAPTER 11
ABOUT THE GOD I SERVE
AND LIVING HOPE

I've been to many funerals, some where the deceased was a follower of Christ, others where the deceased was not a believer. There is a very evident difference in the vibe at each. A funeral for a person who followed Christ tends to have a lighter, hopeful vibe, while a funeral for a person who didn't follow Christ has a heavier, sadder feel to it. This chapter is not to convince you one way or the other or to say that you are doing things wrong. This chapter is simply to tell you about the God that I serve, the God that my wife served, and the hope that we have that goes beyond the grave.

Jesus was a teacher above all other teachers and taught in such a way that no one had ever heard anything close to it. His wisdom was far greater than that of any other person. His dedication to the Father was more disciplined than that of the greatest person to ever roam the earth. Jesus's ability to read the situation was something to admire. You may say that it was easy for Jesus because Jesus was God, and He used those "God" abilities because God is omniscient (all-knowing), omnipresent (all-present), and omnipotent (all-powerful). While Jesus, also known as the Son of God, one person of the Trinity (Father,

Son, and Spirit), was God, He was fully human as well. I know it's difficult to comprehend because we think in terms of one or the other. If I asked my four-year-old son what my name is, he would tell me "Daddy." While that is what he calls me, that is only one of the things that I am called. I am also called Seth, son, brother, cousin, friend, minister, author, and the list goes on and on. When I tell my son that my actual name is Seth, his mind is blown. I think it's the same way when we think of Jesus as God and Jesus as human. This is one of the grand mysteries of our faith—the fact that Jesus was both fully divine and fully human. Our minds are blown when we think about this, right? To help us better understand how Jesus's time on earth as God incarnate worked, I want to further introduce the Holy Spirit. Jesus, fully human yet still fully God, worked in tandem with the Holy Spirit throughout His earthly life and ministry.

The Holy Spirit is the third person of the Trinity: Father, Son, and Holy Spirit. The Spirit serves as an intercessor between people and God. People are sinful by nature and need an intercessor. Jesus triumphed over sin and promised that the gift of the Holy Spirit would be available to people (John 15:26). What's amazing about this gift is not just that we can receive it but that we have a prime example of what it looks like to allow the Spirit to lead in our lives. Jesus had full access to the Holy Spirit (John 3:34), and He let the Spirit lead Him. We tend to look at the life of Christ and see what He did and believe it was easy for Him to do those things; it was quite the opposite. Jesus's human nature had all the same components as ours, but He did very specific things to overcome human nature.

Jesus regularly pulled away from others to seek out communion with the Father. In fact, immediately before Jesus was arrested, He was in the garden of Gethsemane praying and struggling with what was before Him (Luke 22:41–44). Jesus was disciplined and intentional about prayer (Luke 5:16). He allowed the Spirit to work through Him (Acts 10:37–38). He regularly waited for God's timing in His ministry (John 7:6–8). He listened for God's prompting during His earthly life. We learn that He was guided by the Spirit into the desert where He faced temptation (Luke 4:1). When Jesus first started His ministry here on earth, He was baptized, and the Holy Spirit came upon and rested on Him (Matthew 3:16–17). From His conception (Matthew 1:18) to His resurrection (Romans 8:10–11), we find the Holy Spirit working in Jesus's life.

The very special thing about this Holy Spirit is that the very same Spirit who was with Jesus and aided Him in His ministry is for you and for me. We can have that same Spirit within us. We can have the communion with the Father that Jesus had because of the Holy Spirit. Granted, our relationship with the Holy Spirit may look different from the one Jesus had. Jesus lived a sinless life; His life without sin allowed a perfect union with the Spirit. We are sinful people, but that same Spirit still is available to us because of Jesus. Our relationship with the Spirit will be different, but it provides for a communion and intimacy with God that is unmatched on this earth.

The fact is that we live in a world that is full of hate, anger, greed, selfishness, sadness, destruction, and horror. Our God is the opposite of those things. He is a God of love, grace, and redemption. Those things are tough to find in our society at times. Now, we do have good things in this world, but I believe we can find common ground in that this world can be hard to live in. We have things like sickness and tragedy and are expected to get through it. For me, there has only been one way that I've been able to get through my loss, and it centers on my faith and the hope that I have beyond death. Is the death of a loved one easy? No. Is tragedy something that I desire? No. Can I make it through tragedy? Yes.

There are some accounts in the Bible that I like to read and reread. They bring hope that people can work through their tough times and remain faithful to the God they serve. There is the story of Shadrach, Meshach, and Abednego. The king of that time built this huge statue in his image and anytime the king's music was played, all in that kingdom had to bow before the statue and recognize the king as god. These guys weren't having that. The king got angry, had a furnace heated up many times hotter than normal, and said that if they didn't do what he commanded, he'd have them thrown into the furnace (Daniel 3:8–15). Shadrach, Meshach, and Abednego's response is bold and something I think about often as I encounter tough times.

> King Nebuchadnezzar, we do not need to defend ourselves before you in this matter. If we are thrown into the blazing furnace, the God we serve is able to deliver us from it, and he will deliver us from Your Majesty's hand. But even if he does not, we want you to know, Your Majesty, that we will not serve your gods or worship the image of gold you have set up. (Daniel 3:16–18)

How awesome is that response? Essentially, they acknowledged God's ability to save them from whatever they were threatened with or about to go through, but *even if he didn't* save them, they would remain faithful. That's powerful! God did save them though (Daniel 3:19–27). That fiery furnace was so hot that the guys who had to get close enough to throw them in died. There are troubling times when what I want doesn't always match what God has planned, but God is always near and always able. I tend to find myself learning in the times that I still have to enter the fiery furnace. I learn about myself, my faith, and how God still provides in big ways in the midst of tragedy. What great faith that Shadrach, Meshach, and Abednego possessed!

I'm reminded of a time when a Roman soldier, a centurion, came before Jesus with a request to heal his servant. Jesus said that He'd go to this guy's house, and the soldier responded with something like, "You don't even need to bother yourself with coming to my house. You can just speak it, and he will be healed." Jesus was amazed by that guy's response. What great faith that Gentile had! Jesus did speak it, and the servant was healed (Luke 7:2–10).

I'm reminded of another time when a leper came before Jesus and said, "Lord, if you are willing, you can make me clean" (Luke 5:12). Jesus said, "I am willing," and he healed the man (Luke 5:13). What great faith that man had to come to Jesus, recognizing His power and authority over sickness and life's troubles.

I'm reminded of when some friends of a paralytic tore open a hole in the roof of a house where Jesus was teaching to lower the man to the feet of Jesus. They interrupted everything for this man to be healed by Jesus. What great faith the man and his friends had that Jesus could heal him. Jesus told the paralytic to pick up his mat and walk, and the man was healed (Luke 5:17–26).

I'm reminded of a time when Jesus took the long route to his destination and ended up in the region of the Gerasenes. A man who was possessed, dirty, destructive, and naked among the tombs near where Jesus and his disciples docked came up crying out to him. It wasn't the man but the demons that possessed him who were crying out to Jesus. They were the first to acknowledge Jesus as Son of the Most High God. They feared him. They were right to fear him. Jesus healed the man (Luke 8:26–39). What great power Jesus had!

I'm also reminded of an account in the Bible where an innocent man was put on trial without committing a crime. I believe He was technically found not guilty by the person in charge (John 19:4–6), but peer pressure overwhelmed the one giving the verdict. At one point or another in His life, He was betrayed by His own people, His own family, and His own disciples. He was stripped of all clothing and garments. His dignity was forcefully taken from Him. He was beaten. He was spat on. He was broken. He was probably unrecognizable to most. A crown of thorns was placed onto His skull, and He was mocked publicly. Long nails went through the wrists of His outstretched arms in order to secure Him to a piece of wood. A long nail went through His feet into another piece of lumber. Those two pieces of wood were secured together, and that cross with an unrecognizable, innocent man secured to it was erected from the ground. He would die of suffocation on those two pieces of wood as He wasn't able to keep His body elevated enough to get adequate air into His lungs. Crowds stood and cheered at the sight of this innocent man dying. They split up His possessions in front of Him. All of this was done, yet He did not curse. He did not bow down before another god. He did cry out to God though. This innocent man was Jesus (John 18:1–19:37).

We see Jesus cry out, "My God, my God, why have you forsaken me?" (Matthew 27:46). Why did God turn his back on Jesus, His Son? Maybe Jesus was asking that question. Maybe, though, Jesus was crying out a verse from the Psalms of David. Psalm 22 starts out with

> My God, my God, why have you forsaken me?
>   Why are you so far from saving me,
>   so far from my cries of anguish?
> My God, I cry out by day, but you do not answer,
>   by night, but I find no rest. (Psalm 22:1–2)

I challenge you to read the rest of Psalm 22 right now.

We find a fulfillment of David's messianic Psalm 22 in the death of the Messiah. But why would Jesus cry out to God in such a way? Why did Jesus use these words to call out God for forsaking him, turning His back on Him? I think this is where we see our humanity begin to recognize Jesus's humanity. We understand pain. We understand sorrow. We understand rejection. We understand sadness. Some of us live in those things daily. When we see and hear Jesus's words before His death, we relate and have compassion; we understand the struggle. What we don't understand is that while this can be interpreted as Jesus feeling those very same things and crying out in frustration and rejection, it may be Him also recognizing that only God could deliver us from such trials and circumstances. As Jesus used His voice for the last time, crying out to God, He pointed to that psalm that also sees God on the throne, God as strength, God as rescuer, God as one who should be praised, God as the one who satisfies, and God as righteous. What great faith Jesus had in the Father even as He was nailed to a wooden cross!

God could have saved my wife. Just because God didn't save Carol doesn't mean I bow to another. There may be a time when I know why Carol died at a young age, but just because tragedy is around me and I am confused as to why things happen doesn't mean that I live outside what I believe to be true. I cry out.

Yet as I have matured in my faith, I cry out knowing that God works in great and awesome ways even when silence is what I hear. The God that I serve (the same God that Carol served) is a God who has proven to me that He shows up in my life on a daily basis. His will and my desire may not always align, and there are instances that I definitely do not understand how He is working, but that doesn't negate that He alone remains on the throne. He is our strength and rescuer and should be praised. Only His love satisfies because He is righteous—that is the God that we serve.

While the account of Jesus dying for what He knew was true is amazing, if that were the end of it, then it would all be for nothing. What came next, after His death, is where we find our hope.

"He is not here; he has risen" (Matthew 28:6).

And with those words, we find the account of Jesus's resurrection. This is what Jesus had been talking about throughout the Gospels (Matthew, Mark, Luke, and John). No one understood the things that Jesus said were to come before, but they did after the resurrection. When Jesus died, all their hopes and dreams died with Him. They thought it was over. Many of them went into hiding. Their world was crushed. They didn't understand why Jesus allowed Himself to be arrested, tried, and killed. They didn't know why Jesus went through so much torture, pain, and suffering. He did it for us. Jesus had to conquer death for us to have hope—not just hope but "a living hope" as it's described in 1 Peter 1:3–6.

> Praise be to the God and Father of our Lord Jesus Christ! In his great mercy he has given us new birth into a living hope through the resurrection of Jesus Christ from the dead, and

into an inheritance that can never perish, spoil or fade. This inheritance is kept in heaven for you, who through faith are shielded by God's power until the coming of the salvation that is ready to be revealed in the last time. In all this you greatly rejoice, though now for a little while you may have had to suffer grief in all kinds of trials.

Humanity has hope of a forever with God in heaven because of Jesus's resurrection and conquering of death. For this to happen, God the Father had to allow His son to go through pain and suffering. For this to happen, Jesus accepted His role as Savior and took on that pain and suffering. For this to happen, a very able Father who could have saved His Son had to give up His one and only Son. For this to happen, Jesus had to allow Himself to be led by the Spirit. For this to happen, Jesus had to be disciplined, intentional, and deliberate with His actions, thoughts, words, compassion, and love. For this to happen, God the Father, God the Son, and God the Holy Spirit had to love the world so much that anything would be done to save it.

All of that was done, and heaven is a reality for all who accept Christ as the leader of their lives. Hope is that faith, belief, and confident expectation of what is yet to come. Heaven is that hope beyond death and beyond this world. This world is fading and temporary, but heaven is forever.

The funeral for a follower of Christ really is different from one for someone who did not follow Christ. This is not a judgment but the reality of what I've experienced and seen. At the funeral of a follower of Christ, hope fills the room because we serve a God who went to great lengths for us to join Him in heaven. That is where my wife is at. My wife is experiencing the glory of God. She sees her Savior face-to-face. I have no doubt about that.

I do hope and pray that the gospel (the good news that Jesus came from heaven, lived a sinless life, died on a cross to take away our sins, and was not found in that tomb because He had risen and that all who believe and accept Him as Christ and leader of their lives will be able to take part in that inheritance in heaven) leads you to further examine what you believe.

July 1, 2021

Having been serving in ministry for twenty years in some form or fashion, I've seen a lot of things.

I've seen people take their last breath.

I've witnessed families break due to the loss of a loved one.

I've seen wives cry over their husband's bodies and husbands weep over their wives.

I have even seen people argue or bash one another during the open mic/memories portion at a funeral.

I have consoled people facing terminal illness. I have prayed over the sick. I have delivered the news to a loved one that one of their family members have passed.

I have been to funerals with hope and some without.

I've walked the hospital halls. I've sat in many waiting rooms. I've walked people through some of their worst times.

Despite all of that, I wasn't prepared.

I wasn't prepared for my wife's final day on earth. I wasn't prepared for her to take her last breath. I wasn't prepared for the pain. I wasn't prepared to leave my bride at the hospital. I wasn't prepared for my dad to be the one in the passenger seat beside me instead of Carol going home.

I wasn't prepared to tell her parents that they lost their little girl. I wasn't prepared to tell my family that she was gone.

I wasn't prepared to have to tell my boys that Mommy wasn't coming home to them. I wasn't prepared for my oldest son's reaction to that news.

I wasn't prepared to tell Carol's friends that they won't be talking to her anymore. I wasn't prepared to announce to the world that my best friend was gone.

I wasn't prepared to have to clean the house. I wasn't prepared to have to answer questions like, "Where are the boys' sheets?" I wasn't prepared for Carol to not make banana bread with the overly ripe bananas on the counter.

I wasn't prepared for the million little decisions that I would have to make once she passed.

I just wasn't prepared for any of that.

I don't know if you can be prepared for any of that . . .

When tragedy surrounds us, it feels as if you are all alone.

As I look back, even though I knew it then and with each step, I see how God continued to help us along. I see how He has equipped His people to be prepared to take care of others in times like these.

I see how immediately people were by my side. I see how my family surrounded us. I see how people just showed up at the camp to help. I see how each day there is another person asking how they can help. Churches that I've never been to have been calling. People that I never met showed up for the funeral. Whether it was because they know me, the boys, or Carol or just because they felt it the right thing to do, we have been surrounded by others prepared to help however needed.

I guess I wasn't prepared for that either.

Thank you for that.

As it was important for us to have a celebration of life for Carol, it is also important for us to use Carol's life to spread the gospel. I believe that she would want that.

If you attended the service, I hope you left knowing a little more of who Carol was and of her faith.

While I was not prepared for pretty much everything that has taken place the last two weeks, there are a few things that I am prepared to do . . .

I am prepared to speak of things that give me hope.

I am prepared to tell you of the God that Carol and I serve.

I am prepared to tell you that Jesus died for you and conquered death and that our forevers don't have to be looked at without hope.

I am prepared to sit down with you and speak more of Jesus and how my decision to follow Him has changed my life.

I am prepared to let you know that God is love.

I am prepared to also let you know that God is available to you the same as He is to me and was to Carol.

I am prepared to tell you that heaven is real. I am not a "hellfire and brimstone preacher," but if I am prepared to speak of the forever of heaven, I have to mention the forever of a place absent of God.

God's grace is so good though. God's grace and love are stronger than any failure that we own.

I also am prepared to tell you that living out your faith is hard; sometimes we fail. I know I fail.

I also am prepared to walk alongside you as you live out your faith.

I am prepared to tell you that there will be a day when we will fully know the presence of God and not just the fraction of a fraction that we may experience here in this fading world.

We have very few "sure things" in this world.

What I am discovering over these last two weeks is that the things that I am most sure about and the things that I am prepared for are bigger than you and I.

The things that I am most unsure and least prepared for are of this world. I could not imagine going through this terrible time in my life without the hope that rests in Christ.

I also want to thank you for not letting us go through this alone.[12]

Reflection: Changed Forevers

May blessings rain down on you as you search for answers and meaning to what has happened around you. When tragedy strikes, we can get so caught up in pointing fingers and blaming others that we neglect to seek out how God is working around us. As you continue your journey through grief, I challenge you to allow yourself time to also seek out what good God is doing in your life right now.

The disciples didn't know what was going on when Jesus allowed Himself to be arrested. All they knew was that their teacher gave Himself up as an innocent man to be taken into custody. It was an arrest that eventually led to Jesus's death. The disciples weren't sure what to do. Some hid from the guards. Others followed Jesus at a distance. After Jesus was crucified, they all went into hiding. Little did they know that God was working on something so big it would change their forevers.

Right now, your life here on earth may have tragically changed with the loss of a loved one. I pray, though, that in this time, you seek out Christ as the leader of your life as He alone can change your forever!

I am worn out from sobbing.
  All night I flood my bed with weeping,
    drenching it with my tears.
My vision is blurred by grief;
  my eyes are worn out because of all my enemies.

Go away, all you who do evil,
  for the LORD has heard my weeping.
The LORD has heard my plea;
  the LORD will answer my prayer.

— Psalm 6:6–9 NLT

CHAPTER 12
ABOUT THIS GRIEF

About this grief . . .

There is just something about grief that brings wrenching pain but offers healing with the same tear.

I despise grief and loathe its very existence because it's only there because my loved one is not.

But I know deep down in my soul that my journey through grief is what will provide a path into my future.

About this grief . . .

Sometimes I yelled at God, and other times I begged for His comfort.

In the depths of loneliness, I felt very little that would comfort me.

His rod and His staff felt far from me.

I saw no green pastures or quiet waters, and my soul felt burdened.

I could not see past my feelings and fear—they darkened my path.

About this grief . . .
Many times, I've sat at her grave, questioning why she is
gone.
In my heart, I still don't know.
My mind tells me that there is a reason for all of it.
Yet anything good is hard to find—just dark valleys.

About this grief . . .
It's a hard road to travel.
Grief follows tragedy.
It's as if a table was prepared for me, yet my enemies came
and stole my joy.
I was left to pick through the scraps of what was and still
called on to find joy.

About this grief . . .
I have felt many things on my journey through grief.
Nothing has been easy.
It's hard work to grieve.
It's exhausting to mourn.
You feel alone on the journey.
But
God was there.
I just didn't know that I saw Him.

About this grief . . .
He was there as I sat beside that hospital bed.
He was there in the empty chair.
He was there at the funeral.
He was there as I laid in bed weeping.
He was there as I was wrought with loneliness.

He was there when I told our loved ones of our loss.
He was there as I comforted my crying child.
He was there through it all.
He was there when I didn't see Him.
He was there when I didn't feel Him.
He was there when I didn't seek Him.
He was there.
He was there in my grief.

Oh, about this grief . . .
It is a journey that no one wants to travel.
A journey with many paths to choose from, but not all
paths lead to healing.
Denial is one path to take, but it only leads so far; there is
no future in denial.
Anger is a path that only leads to greater heartache; anger
hardens the softest hearts.
Sadness is an easy path to choose, a path that outsiders
easily sympathize with and understand, but it leads only
to deeper sadness if traveled too long.
Depression is the secret path, a path that has connecting
routes to each of the other paths and quickly binds them
together as one and the same if one is not alert—that is a
heavy road to walk.

About this grief . . .
But then there is joy.
The path of joy, even in the darkest grief, shines brighter
than all other paths.

Joy exists even when sadness, anger, denial, and
depression seem to overwhelm you and take hold of
your very being.
Finding joy allows sadness to be lighter.
Finding joy allows anger to flee.
Finding joy allows denial to accept reality.
Finding joy offers moments of freedom from depression,
even if just for a single moment.

Finding joy illuminates the provision given when all
seems lost.

About this grief . . .
It is a process.
This grieving process is exhausting.
It is terrifying.
It is not easy.
It is different for everyone but difficult all the same.
But it is healing.
I find joy despite grief because His rod and His staff were
close to me through the church that surrounded me.
I find joy despite grief because He did lead me beside
quiet waters through my family who has walked alongside
me.
I find joy despite grief as He navigates grief with me,
guiding me into His very righteousness—where my loved
one now finds rest.
I find joy despite grief as I am walking through one of my
darkest valleys because I now see all the times that
He was there.

Now I know He won't ever leave me.

During this grief . . .
I have been comforted.
My cup overflows.
My soul is refreshed.
Because the Lord is my shepherd,
I lack nothing.
Because the Lord is my shepherd.

May joy be found through Him—the one who can satisfy
a weary soul, the one who provides comfort when life
seems wrong, the one who completes the incomplete,
the one who is constant and forever.
May He be found in a friend.
May He be found through the body of Christ—
the church.
May He be found in the smallest of things.
May the grieving know His name—the name of Jesus.
May He be their shepherd as He is mine.
May His name be forever praised.
May our journeys bring glory to the kingdom of God.

NOTES

1. "Carol Anne Tyler of La Monte, MO 1986–2021 Obituary," Sweeney-Phillips & Holdren Funeral Home and Crematory, accessed November 15, 2022, https://www.sweeneyphillipsholdren.com/obituary/carol-tyler.

2. Seth Tyler, "Eleven months. It has been eleven months without Carol," Facebook, May 18, 2021, https://www.facebook.com/sethtyler/posts/pfbid02c5XNpkGnZgry r4i2NEwmg5DQ1aaDVQUT9L99g96VNoiraT3pvg6 waH7pqqGPz4tql.

3. Seth Tyler, "I'm not sure how to do today," Facebook, June 25, 2021, https://www.facebook.com/sethtyler /posts/pfbid0aBLDcF1FS2G1omsmzoauTTnmv8nh3Pf H1ydDfPBsKpuAkeRLxVhmBCZJeFcA2mfBl.

4. Seth Tyler, "Today would have been our thirteenth anniversary," Facebook, August 9, 2021, https://www.facebook.com/sethtyler/posts/pfbid02PwLX4i6tbYP5Yk BQqorPTTnzujgfTjjjMmuym71c7q4VsZJdVNAnJe6vYy 47aCXLl.

5. Nikki, personal communication with author, June 2021.

6. Jen, personal communication with author, June 2021.

7. Dawn, personal communication with author, June 2021.

8. Caroline, personal communication with author, June 2021.

9. Becky, personal communication with author, June 2021.

10. Sarah, personal communication with author, June 2021.

11. Seth Tyler, "Fourteen years ago on August 9th, 2008, Carol Crowe married Seth Tyler," Facebook, August 9, 2022, https://www.facebook.com/sethtyler/posts/pfbid0U LfuXma8ZE1Qd8rrmk1cq3C1QaYK29FZzoUjeZwen ZZBGnysakPYsmCKK5rZHSH8l.

12. Seth Tyler, "Having been serving in ministry for twenty years in some form or fashion," Facebook, July 1, 2021, https://www.facebook.com/sethtyler/posts/pfbid031FR tscXLoShsUEYqFAcRv2JzDqsFMHumiAWBS44hX9 RcGQKrDq3ppttA6jk92Rbl.

Made in the USA
Columbia, SC
20 July 2023

20574267R00098